To Mell and Clive

With love

Peter xx

Stop Me If I've Told You This Before

Stop Me If I've Told You This Before

Peter Bourke

First published in Great Britain in 2021 by
Dream Publishing

Edited, designed and produced by Tandem Publishing
http://tandempublishing.yolasite.com

ISBN: 978-1-5272-9627-5

10 9 8 7 6 5 4 3 2 1

A CIP catalogue record is available from the British Library.

Printed and bound in Great Britain by CPI Group (UK) Ltd, Croydon CR0 4YY.

To Nicky Henson, for forty years
of friendship and laughter

PB by Nobby Clark.

Contents

Dear Reader ix

'You must become good at something…' 1

Francis Showering 7

Inter-Action 14

Dr Michael Bourke 23

Keith Floyd & Hedley Goodall 30

Alan Ayckbourn 34

Patricia Routledge 40

The Royal Shakespeare Company centenary season: 1975/76 44

Busking for Arnold 50

General Sir Brian & Lady Nancy Horrocks 55

Alan Bates 63

Nicky Henson 67

Ralph Richardson 77

Roald Dahl 83

Alan Bennett 91
Robert Stephens 96
Gilbert O'Sullivan 100
Michael Denison & Dulcie Gray 104
Terry Donovan & Nobby Clark 110
Ed Mirvish 116
Jacqueline Wilson 120
Barrie Rutter 124
Peter Crouch & Glenda Jackson 129
Bill Fraser 134
Britt: 12,755 and counting 140
Jeffrey Archer & Paul Scofield 147
John Gielgud 155
Margaret Thatcher 159
Endgame 163
Fair Play Theatre Company 172
Algernon Bourke 177
Fifty Years 183

Acknowledgements 187
Picture Credits 189

Dear Reader

THIS IS A lockdown project inspired by a chance remark. I was invited by an old school chum for drinks on the terrace of his house near the Oval. As the fizz flowed he said to his husband, 'Peter has a wonderful story about Roald Dahl – in fact he has a fund of stories.' Then he turned to me and said, 'You should write them down.'

With little or nothing in the diary I had little or no excuse. My method has been to pour a glass of wine at 5pm, sit at my desk, and in no particular order tell the stories. These stories have been heard time and time again by my three girls (in fact each time I get a new audience). 'Oh no, not the *Star Wars* story!' they cry, 'Not Jeffrey Archer's party again!' or 'Please don't tell the one about your night with Margaret Thatcher… Promise you won't talk about your life in a squat in the 60s – please Daddy, no!'

Perhaps now I've written them down I won't have to perform them again – at least not too often. I have simply tried to write about the people who have interested me. You don't have to read them all – just the ones that interest you.

—Peter Bourke

The Oresteia, Epidaurus, 1982.

'You must become good at something...'

Jack Meyer founded Millfield School with funds from the parents of six Indian princes he had tutored privately. They came to Street, in Somerset, and were taught in Nissen huts. Gradually 'Boss', as he was nicknamed, built an international school around them. At one time in the 60s, when I joined, well over 50 per cent of the pupils were on scholarships. These scholarships were awarded for something the pupil was good at – any sport, any subject – and the way it worked was through Boss Meyer interviewing all students and parents before negotiating their fees.

My sister had been very unhappy at her school and my parents took her away and arranged an interview at Millfield. I went too, having failed my Common Entrance exam. I was sent to a man called

Jack Meyer.

Mr Livy-Noble, in Marlborough, for an intelligence test. He decided that I was intelligent enough, after asking me to name as many objects as I could in two minutes – I just went around his study naming everything I could see. More importantly he discovered that I was dyslexic and later helped me with that, prescribing eye exercises to concentrate on looking from left to right without flicking backwards and forwards, thereby reading the letters in the correct order.

At my sister's interview Boss said to our father, 'I imagine you earn about £4,000 a year. How about £1,000 for both children?' Then he said to Sarah, 'You must become good at something. What is your favourite sport?'

'I don't like sport – but I wouldn't mind doing archery.'

Within a year of taking it up, my sister became Somerset Junior Archery champion. That was the ethos of the school: find something you're good at and everything else will follow.

The scholarships were funded by wealthy parents, such as Elizabeth Taylor, who paid for her two sons, the Wilding boys, and six more. When Lew Grade wanted to send his children, Boss said 'They can come here for free as soon as you've built us a television studio.' He attracted students from all over the world.

As a day boy I used to travel home on the bus with Salem Bin Laden and Bob Howe, who were both in a boarding house in Glastonbury. On Parents' Day Salem's seven wives (at the age of eighteen!) visited him at the George and Pilgrim in Glastonbury. With chronic acne and no girlfriend, I was very jealous. Salem's father was blind and was led around by his two principal wives; Salem was the oldest son of the principal wife, and therefore his heir. At the time, in 1966, his father owned American Airlines and American Electric. Salem became the head of the family when his father died in a plane crash in 1967. Had Salem not himself died in a plane crash in 1988 Osama bin Laden would not have come into his inheritance. Bob Howe was Stanley Howe's son, Stanley Howe of Howe's Bank, Hong Kong, who owned all the gambling on the island of Macau.

Also on Parents' Day, Hayley Mills would come and visit her brother John, and David Brown would drive up in his latest Aston Martin, to the delight of us boys in particular.

There were no rules at the school so you were expected to discipline yourself. Many of the staff were retired from jobs at other schools: Anthony Chenevix-Trench taught us English – he had been the headmaster of Eton. David Cornwell, otherwise known as John Le Carré, also taught English.

The classes were very small. On one occasion there were just three of us in Remedial Maths, waiting for our tutor, who was late. I asked the boy on my left what he wanted to do when he left school. 'I want to be a film producer,' he replied. I asked him how he'd go about doing that. 'I'm going to start by being a film editor – that's where all film happens.' A couple of years later I bumped into him in Soho Square, carrying a tin of film. I saw him at a party, I saw him at a swimming pool in Shepherd's Bush, and eventually I saw Jeremy Thomas climbing onto the podium to collect an Oscar for *The Last Emperor*. The other schoolfellow was Nick Daubeny, who also went into film, and picked up a BAFTA for location management, once managing to shut down the whole of the centre of London for a film shoot.

Boss Meyer promised parents 'I *will* find something your child is good at' – he had a unique knowledge of all of us. While he had been in India, it was said that he'd learnt a yoga technique that allowed him to sleep for only seven minutes a day. I remember going to ask him if I could take a girl called Penny Morgan to the cinema on Saturday night. As I asked the question he fell asleep and Miss Sanky, his secretary, said 'Don't worry, he won't be long.' Seven minutes later he woke up and said yes.

Boss was a gambler: a girl I had a huge crush on was at Millfield because Boss had lost the school fees to her father at Monte Carlo. The father used to turn up in a helicopter and take people for rides to raise money for school funds. One year I asked the girl why her father hadn't come to Parents' Day.

'He can't afford to.'

'What about the helicopter?'

'He lost it in a card game.'

'So where is he?'

'Still in Monte Carlo.'

In each of our small classes, you could choose what subjects to study and you could choose your tutor by going around the staff with your week planner. Looking back, it was an extraordinary, free-wheeling experience, run on a sort of Robin Hood, robbing the rich to pay the poor, system. In the end, the governors of the school lost patience with Boss and forced him to retire.

This he was not happy about and left for a gambling binge in London, where he announced that he had been obliged to give up Millfield. 'But I still have many years left to create the perfect international school, ideally on a Greek island.' That night he raised the funds he needed and went on to found a school in Athens, St Lawrence College, that he ran for many more years.

Francis Showering

Francis Showering was a patient of my father's. He and his three brothers ran a cider pub on the High Street in Shepton Mallet. They also had a brass quartet – they were 'players'.

In 1950, when I was born, Francis and his girlfriend Hilda used to babysit me. It was their way of being on their own together.

One year in the late 1950s there was an excellent pear crop in Somerset and Francis decided to make cider from them – basically, that became Babycham. He hired an advertising man, Jack Wynne-Williams, who came up with the slogan 'I'd love a Babycham,' with a cartoon drawing of a chamois dancing on a champagne-style glass, which held a cherry on a stick.

It became England's top-selling drink, but not before Francis had insisted that each of his brothers

put their houses up as collateral so that he could buy additional vats to cope with the demand that he anticipated after the ad was launched.

Not content with the phenomenal success of Babycham, Francis took his brothers on a spending spree, buying Bird's Custard, Kiwi Shoe Polish, Beechams Powders, Britvic and finally Harveys, famous for Harveys Bristol Cream sherry.

I remember many wonderful occasions when we, as a family, were lavishly entertained by Francis and his wife (as she became) Hilda. They had bought a beautiful house on the Beaulieu River called Fiddlers. They had a butler and housekeeper, gardeners and people to tend the heated swimming pool. Moored at the end of the garden was a luxury yacht, built by Silvers boatyard on the Clyde and launched by my mother – an occasion we all attended, travelling on the sleeper to Glasgow after dinner in the Pinafore Room at the Savoy.

We would spend days on the yacht, sailing round the Isle of Wight and lunching on board after mooring at Cowes. My mother and father often holidayed with Francis and Hilda, sailing to Holland and through the canals, always stopping for the night near wonderful restaurants. Dad always paid for one of the meals – the bill often came to as much as the price of a package holiday.

Before one of the dinners at Fiddlers the butler poured champagne. Francis turned to my father and said, 'What do you think of this, Michael? It's called Taittinger – I think it's a lovely everyday champagne.' Then at dinner he said, 'What about this? I think it's the finest red wine I've ever tasted and I'm going to put it on the map.' It was Château Latour – both the red wine and the champagne were part of the package he had bought as Harveys.

He also bought J. Lyons and Co, and reinstated a Lyons' Corner House opposite Charing Cross Station on the Strand, now sadly a Pizza Express.

But the anecdote I want to tell has nothing and everything to do with Francis's business acumen. Because he was wealthy, the organisers of the Mid-Somerset Show in Shepton Mallet, the forerunner of the Bath and West, called Francis and asked him to be their President. It was 1964 and they had debts.

'All right,' said Francis, 'but I will only do it for a year.'

In that year he set out to find an attraction to bring in the crowds. He rang Brian Epstein, the Beatles's manager, and asked him how much it would cost for them to perform. 'Do you know how much he asked for??!!' he said later, 'I told him I certainly wasn't having them!' So on every journey he made in his Rolls-Royce he listened to pop music, seeking advice from his nephews and nieces, and for £100 booked an emerging group called the Small Faces. As their Bedford van drove into the showground they were number one on *Top of the Pops*. The audience was hanging from the rafters and I still remember their lead singer, Steve Marriott, strutting his stuff on a makeshift stage in the main show ring, surrounded by jumps.

Needless to say, Francis Showering paid off the Mid-Somerset Show's debts and earned them a tidy profit. When Showerings amalgamated with Allied Breweries in the 1970s, Francis personally was worth £128 million, and Babycham was still their best-selling drink. Later, in 1982, when his nephew Keith died unexpectedly of a heart attack (in the Bank of England), Francis was asked to take his place on the board and to be Vice Chair of Allied Breweries.

When Hilda died, Francis married his secretary, Rita, and left the house he had built behind the Babycham factory. There he had kept chamois in a field, where he also allowed my sister Sarah and I to keep our ponies.

Francis was a wise man, and a kind man, with a great sense of humour. My father often visited him after he retired. He became nearly blind as a result of diabetes, but still kept his drive. On one of my father's visits Francis took him to the fridge and out came a jam jar.

'What does that say, Michael?'

'Straight Eight,' my father replied.

'Taste it.'

'Delicious.'

Francis had been worried about his nephews, living the millionaire lifestyle in London, and invited them for the weekend. After a fabulous dinner he announced that they were all going into business, him included. 'But Uncle Francis, we're in a recession!'

'Yes, and that's the perfect time to launch a cheap drink. You boys have got to roll your sleeves up and get to work.'

Together they launched Straight Eight and a few months later, when Dad asked how it was going, Francis replied, 'Well, a lot better than Babycham did in its first months, so it hasn't done badly.' Francis had invented the first alcopop and Brothers Drinks is still in business today.

In 1975 Francis built a versatile theatre in Shepton Mallet town centre and asked my mother to open it. It had a tiered auditorium with seats that, with a hydraulic lift, disappeared into the roof leaving a sprung dance floor and a stage for the band. My then wife Kate Nicholls and I performed at the opening, alongside local boy Christopher Cazenove and his wife Angharad Rees, but it very nearly didn't get finished. The costs had over-run by a million pounds and Francis went to his local bank. 'I'm going to need a million-pound loan,' he said, 'until I can get one from the Bank of England.'

'I'll have to let you know tomorrow,' the bank manager said.

That evening Francis was at a cocktail party and asked a friend's son, 'What are you doing these days?'

'Working at the Midland Bank in Shepton Mallet, sir.'

'Really? Well, I have a story for you. I asked my bank to let me have a million pounds to finish the work on the new theatre and do you know what the manager said, "I'll have to let you know tomorrow"!'

'I will get you a million pounds by lunchtime tomorrow, sir.'

'Do you think you can?'

'Yes, sir. If you come to the bank for 12.45 tomorrow I will have it for you.'

'Good luck – see you tomorrow.'

When Francis parked his Rolls outside the Midland Bank at 12.45pm the following day, the young man came down the steps to meet him, with a broad smile. 'I have the million for you, sir.'

That day Francis transferred all of Allied Breweries business to the Midland Bank, and the young man got a promotion. The beautiful Bath stone theatre was opened by my mother cutting the ribbon, with the same flair as when launching two of Francis's yachts, the *Silver Cavalier* and the *Silver Buccaneer*.

As my father said at Francis's funeral, 'He was a great man and I was proud to call him my friend.'

Inter-Action

IN 1968 I was in a National Youth Theatre production of *Macbeth* at the Roundhouse. One weekend during rehearsals I was back home in Shepton Mallet for a wedding. At the reception I got talking to a girl who asked me what I was doing at the moment and I told her about the show. 'You should get in touch with Ed Berman at Inter-Action,' she said. 'They're an arts commune and they do street theatre, workshops in remand homes, all sorts. Their offices are opposite the Roundhouse in Chalk Farm.'

The following week, in a break, I did just that. Ed Berman had read Economics at Harvard and later at Oxford. He had a huge ego and a huge social conscience. Inter-Action was his baby, a registered charity, receiving funds from the Rowntree Trust, the Gulbenkian Foundation and, eventually, the Arts Council. They had a street theatre group called Dogg's Troupe and a show called *Moon Men*, which involved Ed with a megaphone gathering kids to join

Edward Berman (left), 28, an American and leader of the Dogg's troupe of street actors which formed a Santa Claus Union, breaking into song yesterday after he and 11 other members, including three women, had appeared at Marlborough Street charged with obstructing the highway in Oxford Street on Wednesday. They pleaded not guilty and were each remanded on £50 bail until Feb. 10. Some carried their costumes into court.

Ed Berman (L) leading us in protest, 1969.

the cast. There were eight members of Inter-Action and they lived in an organised squat on Malden Road in Kentish Town, next-door to the Simon Community, a safe house for drug addicts.

I walked into the office and said that I would love to come and work for them. Ed asked me what experience I'd had, and I replied that I'd been an assistant stage manager for a year at Lincoln Theatre Royal, run by Philip Hedley and Brian Spiby.

'Can I ring them for a reference?'

'Of course.'

Ed told me to come back the next day when he'd had a chance to give them a call, so the following afternoon I turned up again. 'We weren't able to get hold of either Brian or Philip,' said Ed, 'but we did get hold of the Arts Council trainee director. How did you get on with her?'

'Not very well.'

'Why?'

'Because she teased me about being public school and I got my own back by outing her as also having been to public school, and being the daughter of a Lord.'

Ed laughed: 'I'll tell you what she said about you – she said you were lazy and untalented.'

'Oh,' I said, 'I think I'd better leave.'

'Not at all! A bad reference from someone like her is a good reference to us. When can you start?'

And so I started six months of living in the Malden Road squat, sharing a room full of bunkbeds with Patrick Barlow, Geoff Hoyle and various others. We had £1 a day for subsistence and a rota for cooking, cleaning and washing up.

We improvised shows for the street and produced plays at a lunchtime theatre club in Frith Street, Soho called The Ambience. It was in a restaurant called

The Green Banana, run by actor Norman Beaton. I stage managed these shows and sometimes appeared in them. We opened with *A Who's Who of Flapland* by David Halliwell and the only other play we had was *Striptease*, by Slawomir Mrożek. To avoid paying entertainment tax we had a club licence. Our membership included Lord Goodman, Lord Olivier, Joan Plowright, Vanessa Redgrave and many more. For the £5 membership fee we guaranteed twelve world premieres a year – but we had only the two plays.

Ed Berman had persuaded Tom Stoppard to write a 15-minute *Hamlet* for our troupe, which he did – it became known as *Dogg's Hamlet*. So we asked him if he'd write some one-act plays for us, and he wrote *After Magritte*, *The Real Inspector Hound*, *Dirty Linen* and *Newfound Land*, the last two of which had long runs at the Arts Theatre in the West End.

One day after a lunchtime performance I was clearing up when a six-foot black man wearing a silver jacket and sunglasses to match filled the door. He came in, swung one of the gold and red velvet chairs between his legs and sat down. 'I think the boys would like a drink,' he said to Norman, and as he said this five more men came in. It felt like a scene from a film. 'I think you'd better go, man,' Norman hissed to me. 'Well, if there's nothing more for me to do?' I said nervously, hearing my voice sound even more high-pitched and public school than usual, and ran up the stairs and into Frith Street.

When I came to work the following morning the first thing I saw was Norman's feet poking out from under a table. For a moment I thought he was dead.

'Are you all right, Norman?' I stuttered.

He rolled out: 'Everything's cool, man. No need to worry.'

So I shut up and started changing the basement restaurant back into a lunchtime theatre. This was the late 60s and it wasn't until 1975 in the RSC Green Room at Stratford that I heard the end of that episode. I'd been telling the story when Ben Kingsley suddenly chimed in.

'I went with him.'

'What?'

'I went with Norman and stood on a corner of Frith Street that afternoon with £400 protection money in a briefcase – but nobody ever turned up to collect.'

Norman, who later became the star of *Desmond's* on Channel 4, was involved on the occasion when Whiteleys, the Bayswater department store, approached Ed and Inter-Action to ask us to deliver Father Christmas to the store, gathering kids from the street, for publicity. Ed asked me to accompany him to the meeting of directors in a panelled room on the top floor. We sat down to discuss what they wanted and what Ed thought they should pay – this was Christmas 1968 – 'It's £600 or nothing,' he said. Silence. He got up and walked out of the room, with me trotting behind him.

'That's the way to sell a show.'

'But…'

A voice came from behind us:

'Would you come back please, Mr Berman?'

We returned to our seats.

'You can have £600 but for that we want Father Christmas to arrive on a steam engine.'

Ed agreed and we went back to our squat to start planning rehearsals for a street show that would involve kids from the high-rise blocks and housing estates around Paddington and Bayswater. Songs included 'Santa Claus, ho ho ho' sung to the tune of 'Piccolomini', which was the only tune Ed knew. He was master of ceremonies with his megaphone, we were all dressed in Eskimo costumes and Patrick Barlow was Father Christmas – on a steam engine. We gathered about 100 kids together, singing and dancing all the way to Whiteleys and up through the store to the toy department. There we were stopped by a security guard who said that nobody could come into Santa's Grotto without paying seven shillings and sixpence. Ed made a quick decision to pay the fee for all and we asked each child what they would like from the shelves. 100 toys were distributed to our delighted group, by which time we had spent the whole of our fee.

A lot of children went home happy and we went back to Malden Road, angry about the exploitation of children by big stores at Christmas. There were nine of us, enough to form a union – the Father Christmas Union – and the following day we went to picket Selfridges in Oxford Street, dressed in our costumes and doing our show. We hadn't been there twenty minutes before we were arrested for obstruction, but not before Norman Beaton had been spirited away, the police being keen not to make it a race issue.

We were questioned separately as I believe the police didn't really have anything to charge us with and they hoped our stories would differ. They were looking for something that might hold up in court. The following day we were in Marylebone magistrates' court, where we were swiftly bailed and required to appear two months later.

We had made the 6 o'clock news on the BBC and invited some high-profile theatre people to attend our trial, promising an entertainment. In due course we were tried, all together, wearing our costumes and singing our songs. Guilty! Fined £10 each. The fines were paid for us, as a ticket price for the show, by Tom Stoppard, Vanessa Redgrave, etc.

Earlier that year we had been asked by the ICA, the Institute of Contemporary Arts, to open their studio theatre with a play called *The Pit*, which had premiered at the newly opened Oval House. It was an improvised show under the direction of Naftali Yavin for Inter-Action's TOC troupe – TOC standing for The Other Company. The set was a box, held together with pin hinges, and the flats had holes in them for the audience to see through. It consisted chiefly of dialogue about imagined sex lives, while the actors removed their clothes. Once dressed again, the actors dismantled the set, which stood between them and the onlookers, a section at a time, and confronted the audience:

'What did you get from that?'

'I could see you were breaking down barriers between actor and audience…'

After the first performance I asked a woman in a headscarf what she had made of it.

'Before I answer that, you should know that there are two steps into this theatre. The bottom one is shallow and the top is steep. A blind person coming to your show would fall over on the top step.'

'Thank you, I'll look into that. So what did you get from the show?'

'Do you really want to know?'

'Yes.'

'Well, when you've cleared up I'll see you in the bar.'

When I found her she offered me a cigar.

'Well, this is show business,' I thought.

She asked me if I was thinking of being an actor.

'Yes,' I answered, thinking that was pretty obvious.

'Well,' she said, 'before you abuse the art, learn about it. It is not well known that I trained at RADA and toured for some years before I had the courage to start up theatre workshops.'

It was the great Joan Littlewood, and that afternoon I got on the bus to Gower Street, paid 10 shillings and put my name down to audition for the May intake at RADA.

I saw Joan Littlewood again in Paris in 1980. I was in the National Theatre production of *The Provok'd Wife* at the Odéon for the Comédie-Française. She was accompanied by Baron Philippe de Rothschild, who she introduced as 'This is Philippe, who is the best French to English translator of plays,' not, as we thought of him, a well known wine producer. I reminded her of our first meeting and thanked her for her advice. Of course she didn't remember but she immediately said that she was thinking of doing street theatre in Northern Ireland and would I be interested? 'I certainly would,' I answered. Sadly, it never happened.

Nicky Henson, John Wood, PB and Michael Kitchen in *The Provok'd Wife*, NT, 1980.

Dr Michael Bourke

My father was head of the student drama society at Bristol University when a young Nadine Blandford auditioned for him. Using every family member's ration card, they married in Taunton and honeymooned at the Cumberland Hotel, Marble Arch, London, a few days before my father was posted out as a medical officer, first to Africa and then with African troops to India.

He saw very little action and the worst medical condition he had to deal with was venereal disease. Dad duly sent a request to the War Office for condoms, and got a reply from Winston Churchill himself.

'Dr Bourke, is it true that theirs are bigger than ours?'

'I don't know, Prime Minister, as I haven't seen one aroused.'

In due course my father received a supply of condoms which were extra large and stamped 'British medium size'.

My parents (© Antony Dufort).

Every day during the War my parents exchanged letters, and when the War was over they had a short spell in London while Dad worked at a hospital in Putney, before settling in Shepton Mallet, where he took up general practice at the heart of Aneurin Bevan's National Health Service. This came home to me most poignantly as, at the time of writing this, we had just clapped the NHS for the tenth and last time in our weekly tribute to their fight against the coronavirus.

My father was full of anecdotes of general practice and, on what would have been his 100th birthday, 30 May 2020, I met up with my sister Sarah to reminisce about him and to share a bottle of champagne in celebration of his humour and wisdom and benign influence.

A Dr Brokenhurst had run the practice before Dr

Annie Hyatt, who passed it on to my father and, very pertinent during this pandemic, had seen the fewest deaths in the whole country from the Spanish Flu that raged in 1918. His remedy was to prescribe a nightly tot of whisky to his patients.

One of my favourite stories about Dad was him asking a patient: 'How are your bowels?'

'I beg your pardon, doctor?'

'It's a perfectly normal question – how are your bowels?'

'I'd rather not say, sir.'

'I'm your doctor and I need to know.'

'All right, if you must know, the left one hangs a little lower than the right.'

My father and mother gave my sister Sarah and me an idyllic childhood. The holidays home from boarding school and later from Millfield, where we were day pupils, were spent with our ponies, which were our transport, our playmates and our work. We had a self-appointed gardener called Bill Wiltshire, who had been in charge of horses in the trenches during the First World War. He was wonderful with animals and kept and showed budgerigars. The colour of the budgies' plumage was all-important for these shows and Bill was colour-blind. The first crime I knowingly committed was as his accomplice in enhancing the wing feathers of his prize-winning birds. He would ask me, 'What colour is that?'

'Bright red.'

'Good, open it,' and with a small paintbrush he would deepen the colouring of the bird perching patiently on his finger.

'Is this all right?' I asked him.

'Not according to my Missus, but as I've always said, she should have married a clergyman.'

One day I asked my parents why people got married. 'Well,' said my mother, 'if a person loves another person, they ask them if they will marry them.'

That afternoon, aged four, I went to the vegetable garden and asked Bill Wiltshire to marry me.

'Oh,' said Bill, 'what a wonderful offer.'

Then he thought for a moment and said, 'Peter, if you still feel the same when you're nine, then we shall.'

In 1963, when Bill was dying, my father arranged for him to be taken into the cottage hospital.

'How are the chickens?' asked Bill.

'Not too bad.'

'Are they laying, doctor?'

'A bit.'

'You've got to scold them,' and added, 'from me. Oh, and I'm going to say thank you for all you've done for me, you and Mrs Bourke. And I'm going to say goodbye, as I'm going to go to sleep tonight and not wake up in the morning.'

Which is exactly what he did. And the advice about the chickens worked a treat.

My father always said that he felt so fortunate to be practising at a time of penicillin and antibiotics, which really could work miracles. My first realisation of what my father did was when I was four, and had woken up in the middle of the night to have a pee, only to find my father, fully dressed, coming up the stairs.

'Daddy, what are you doing?'

'Peter, I've just witnessed a miracle. I've just delivered a baby, and every baby is a miracle.'

On one occasion he was called out to a remote farm in the middle of the night and it was snowing so badly that he had to walk over fields to get there, to be met by the farmer.

'It's my daughter, doctor, she's upstairs. But this baby isn't going to live, doctor, is it? You see, the baby's father … my daughter's husband is in the Army … and the baby isn't his, so…'

The baby was delivered, a healthy boy, and my father asked what they were going to name him.

'What's your name?'

'Michael.'

'That's what he can be called then.'

Many years later my father was called to the farmer's bedside. He was very ill with pneumonia.

'How are you managing?' Dad asked.

'Well, doctor, I have this wonderful grandson. He's transformed the farm. He's the best thing that's ever happened to me in my entire life, is Michael.'

Back before my father inherited his practice from Dr Annie Hyatt, who retired in the 50s to marry the editor of the *Shepton Mallet Journal*, he was struggling to make ends meet. He had been making daily visits to a farmer's wife at a big dairy farm near Glastonbury and the farmer said to him, 'Doctor, you've saved my wife's life and she is the most important and valuable thing I have. I want you to have anything you want – look around, you just have to say.'

'I was only doing my job,' replied Dad. 'I really don't need anything.'

'I know what you should have,' said the farmer, clapping his hands and calling his wife, 'something that money can't buy. Missus, fetch the doctor a glass of milk straight from the cow!'

Another patient of my father's was Michael Eavis at Worthy Farm in Pilton. He held a pop concert at his farm one year and called it the Pilton Festival. My father agreed to be there as medical officer. The entrance fee was £1 and for that you got a pint of milk and a rock band – the event was such a success that it grew and grew and became the Glastonbury Festival that we know today.

There are so many stories about my mother and father and his forty-plus years in general practice, culminating in a BBC film for the Open University comparing a country practice to a city practice. My mother managed the reception, waiting room and office, answering the phone, filing records, testing urine samples. All of this was unpaid. She was both his guard dog and his lap dog – they were a great love affair.

In 1967 my parents were despairing about my O level results – just three passes, in Maths, English and Divinity – and about my eventual work prospects. My sister Sarah chirped up: 'You should be an actor – you always said you wanted to be an actor.'

On the following Sunday afternoon we – and I mean we – sat down and wrote, after consulting *The Stage* newspaper, more than sixty letters to the various repertory theatres around the country. The replies were almost all along the lines of: 'We have nothing at the moment but will keep you on file,' but Lincoln Theatre Royal invited me for an interview in London. As a result of that interview, with Philip Hedley (later of Stratford East) and Brian Spiby (later head of drama for BBC TV), I was offered a job as a student assistant stage manager, at £3 a week, with £1 for every four hours of overtime. Overtime started at 2am on a Sunday morning and with a turn-round, 'strike' and set-up normally taking about sixteen hours and touring in and out of four other theatres, in Boston, Scunthorpe, Rotherham and Loughborough, I usually managed to make about £7 a week.

Keith Floyd & Hedley Goodall

IN 1969, AFTER a year as a student assistant stage manager at Lincoln Theatre Royal, and six months at Inter-Action, I was at Weston Technical College in Weston-super-Mare under the pretence of taking A levels – the A levels I had run away from at Millfield.

Although I was living in Weston-super-Mare I used to go to Bristol to work on my audition speeches for RADA with a wonderful old actor called Hedley Goodall. For a case of wine – 'No tax on that' – he said to my father, 'If he's any good I'll get him in.' We worked on two speeches – the 'naming of the dead' speech from *Henry V* and a cobbled-together speech from Arnold Wesker's *Chips with Everything*. When I went to meet him I took my guitar, which in those days I had with me at all times. To relax me, Hedley asked me to play him a song. He listened patiently then said, 'There is a small bistro in Clifton

Keith Floyd at The Maltsters Arms, Tuckenhay.

called Floyds, run by a chap called Keith Floyd. He's looking for a guitarist/singer. Go and see him and tell him I sent you.'

I did as I was told, played for Keith, and he asked me to start right away. I sat on the open staircase and played as background music, then took requests from customers at their tables. Keith was a wonderful host, making everyone feel very welcome, and of course he cooked like a dream. If things were going well he gave people free drinks, kept the place open late – it was a party. He had trained with the Roux

Brothers and told me that his 'audition' was to cook an omelette. Albert Roux had said, 'If you can cook an omelette, you can cook.'

At the end of a long evening at Floyds Bistro, Keith would cook a meal for all the staff and give us wonderful wine. That would have been enough but he also paid me £8, which was a king's ransom in 1969, and sent me home to Weston-super-Mare in a cab at his expense. For years, £8, dinner and a taxi home was the best money I ever earned.

Hedley Goodall said to me before my RADA audition, 'Let your yes be yes and your no be no to any question you are asked.' Good advice, but I think it was also to do with clarity, not saying – as was the way in the 60s – yeah and na. I asked him if he thought I should take my guitar to the audition.

'Have they asked you to?'

True to his word, he got me into RADA for a case of good wine from Avery's. I think the clincher was in the 'naming of the dead' speech, when he suggested that I should be moved by 'Davy Gam, esquire'. I was still using that speech when I auditioned for Terry Hands for the RSC, to play Boy in *Henry V.*

'Why did you choose that speech? You might as well have recited the telephone directory. Try learning the Boy's speech, "As young as I am" and do it for me tomorrow.'

I was staying with Nick Salmon and we had a delicious meal together with a lot of wine and, with my head spinning, I learnt the speech. I woke in the morning and knew it, taking it to my new friend Patricia Routledge, who can phrase a line better than any actor alive. It was a combined effort that got me the job.

Alan Ayckbourn

I MET ALAN Ayckbourn through the radio producer Alfred Bradley, who some say invented radio drama. Alan went to work for Alfred after his first play, *Mr Whatnot*, opened at the Arts Theatre, London, and received unfavourable notices. The Arts Theatre was at the time run by Michael Codron who, after this shaky start, went on to produce all Alan's early successes – at least thirty-seven of them! He had a keen eye for talent, reading early plays by writers including Samuel Beckett, Tom Stoppard and Harold Pinter, producing them at the Arts Theatre, often directed by Peter Hall.

Alfred used to come to all the shows I was in at the Leeds Playhouse, later called the West Yorkshire Playhouse, now the Leeds Playhouse again. After my two years there Alfred said, 'You are in my little black book. When you are next in London, give Alan a call on this number. He lives at 11a Keats Grove in Hampstead and he will be expecting your call.'

I was in London to audition for a television play called *Initiation*, a half-hour play about a bookbinder's apprentice. My audition was with Brian Parker and took some time as we read through the whole play. He knew I was dyslexic so he gave me plenty of time to prepare.

Afterwards I called Ayckbourn from a telephone box in Sloane Square. 'Yes,' he said, 'come and see me at 6 o'clock.' When I entered his beautiful, modern, open-plan house, he offered me a glass of sherry and I thought, 'This is the life.' He started telling me the story of his early years, living in a bedsit in Earl's Court with his wife and baby son. The only flat surface for writing was the top of the Baby Belling stove and the only quiet time was during the night. He had written some pages, left them on the stove and fallen asleep. Later on, only half awake, his wife turned the stove on to heat up their son's bottle of milk and the pages went up in flames – an incident he later used in his play *Woman in Mind*.

Alan said he thought to himself, 'There must be something better than this. We should go and live by the sea, buy cheap fish at the end of the day.' So they moved to Scarborough, where he met Stephen Joseph, who ran a theatre in the round in the local library, and who took him on as his stage manager. While doing that job, Alan questioned Stephen's choice of plays for the coming season. Stephen said, 'If you write a play, I'll put it on.'

At this point, Alan interrupted his flow of reminiscence by asking me if I wanted to try out a couple of speeches. I was taken off-guard and had finished my schooner of sherry so was not as sharp as I would have liked. I asked him if I could use his loo – this was so that I could splash water on my face. As I looked into the mirror I said to myself, 'You can do this.'

So I read for him and afterwards he said, 'What are you in London for?'

'A half-hour play for the BBC,' I told him.

'Oh,' he said, 'I think you've got that. Peter King the playwright has worked with me in Scarborough.'

Alan went on to tell me about the play he wrote for Stephen Joseph, which was called *Meet My Father.* At the first read-through, before rehearsing, Stephen said, 'Cast, please will you put your thumbs in at page x, and forefingers at page y, and take out the pages in between,' (smoke was coming out of Alan's ears) 'and Alan, you can use those pages in another play.' He went on, 'The title's no good. We must change it to *Relatively Speaking.*' It became the first of many many hits for Alan, in Scarborough and then the West End. The rumour was that his first thirty plays made a million each.

At Christmastime Alan called me and offered me a part in his new play, *Bedroom Farce*, for the 1975 summer season in Scarborough, but I was already engaged for the RSC's centenary season. When he offered again, it was in the early nineties.

Alan is a great director of other people's plays as well as his own, and describes his method of directing as 'sheep-dogging' – to get the actor through the right hole in the fence, in the end.

A season with him is exhausting – three shows a day, sometimes while rehearsing another. He believes that you can't overwork an actor, but you can underwork one. If you underwork them they have affairs and break marriages.

He writes a play in a fortnight, that has been gestating for a year, often announcing the title before writing the play. He used to have a cigarette after every page he wrote, then, when he gave up smoking, his wife Heather was always 'on call' with a sandwich.

He says of his plays, 'I mine the same six characters all the time,' but when he wrote about a Finn in a play about a firework party (starring Christopher Cazenove) the director Casper Wrede, from the Royal Exchange Theatre in Manchester, said 'That's me, isn't it?'

'No,' said Alan.

'Hang on,' replied Casper, 'How many Finns do you know?'

Alan's mother brought him up and she made her living out of freelance journalism, for newspapers and magazines. When I finally worked for Alan, and when his mother came to shows, it was like a visit from the Queen Mother. His father had been the lead violinist of the Hallé Orchestra and was a largely absentee dad, so Alan was sent to board at an English public school, Haileybury College.

When I worked for him he directed me in a play he had written for children called *My Very Own Story.* He loved writing for children but his bank manager encouraged the adult plays. His adult play that season was *Wildest Dreams,* also a West End success.

Alan Ayckbourn is a master of his craft and, like Noël Coward, makes audiences laugh at themselves, thinking they are laughing at their neighbours. When he got his knighthood, he had waited to divorce his first wife before marrying Heather, so that he could make them both Lady Ayckbourn. I leapt for joy when he was given that knighthood – comedy is not taken seriously enough!

Patricia Routledge

My early theatre-going was at the Bristol Old Vic, which had two theatres. My favourite was the little and beautiful Georgian theatre, where you were greeted by a man in evening dress who made you feel very welcome, showing you down the passageway to the perfect auditorium. The smell, the excitement! I saw everything – if my parents were paying – from the best seats in the stalls; if I was with friends, spending our own pocket money, up in the gods.

I saw Peter O'Toole's Hamlet. I saw *Who's Afraid of Virginia Woolf*; my father took me and my sister Sarah without having done his research beforehand. We loved it, and got rather more from it than Daddy, who felt embarrassed to have brought us, and thought he was attracting stares from other members of the audience. And it was where I saw Patricia Routledge for the first time, as the ghost of Sarah Siddons in the Julian Slade show *Christmas in King Street*.

My next exposure to this glorious actress was with Alastair Sim in Pinero's *The Magistrate*, while I was a drama student. I was taken by my landlady, Jennifer Porteous, also an actress, as an example of how it should be done. Imagine my excitement when I was cast as Traddles in the BBC Sunday afternoon classic series of *David Copperfield* and found that Patricia was playing Mrs Micawber, with the great Arthur Lowe as Mr Micawber. I was in a trance at early rehearsals.

Arthur's great line was 'To fall back as it were, before what I hope I will not be accused of presumption in presuming a spring' – all this delivered as he leant back, holding a bottle, leaning forward to pour as he said 'spring'.

Patricia was wonderful, and her most memorable line came in her final speech, which now seems prophetic: 'This land I have come to conquer. Have ye riches, have ye honours, let them be brought forward – they are mine!'

Pat was a star in America, on Broadway, before we worked together, winning a Tony Award no less. We came together again for the BBC's *Nicholas Nickleby*; she was Mrs Mantalini and I was Smike. Later on there was the television comedy series *Marjorie and Men*, and the nine-month West End hit run of Priestley's *When We Are Married*, directed by the great Ronald Eyre.

Making friends is destiny, and we have been friends, for better or worse, for nearly half a century. Pat has been there for all the major events in my and my family's lives – birthdays, baptisms, weddings, graduations, funerals. She has travelled from her home in Chichester to Salisbury, Scarborough, Derby, Sheffield, Colchester and London to attend my performances.

Her own career is legendary: the Victoria Wood monologues, the Alan Bennett monologues, the world-sweeping success of Hyacinth Bucket in *Keeping Up Appearances*. Then there were the great stage performances: Mad Margaret in *Richard III*, Lady Bracknell in *The Importance of Being Earnest* and the wonderful show she now takes on tour, *Entrance One Shilling*, with Piers Lane at the

COWLEY'S WEEKEND WINNER

Captain turns con-man

DICKENS characters have never been fruitier than they are in his unnerving NICHOLAS NICKLEBY (BBC 1, Sunday, 5.0). This six-parter, dramatised by the excellent Hugh Leonard, has plum parts for Nigel Havers as Nicholas, Derek Godfrey (Captain Holt in 'Warship') as con-man Uncle Ralph, Derek Francis as the appalling Wackford Squeers, tyrant of that most loathsome of Dickensian boarding schools, Dotheboys Hall, and Peter Bourke (pictured right) as the devastated wretch, Smike. More fine character actors are waiting in the wings. Stay tuned.

piano. Not to mention her appearances in musicals: award-winning performances on Broadway in Styne and Harburg's *Darling of the Day*, as the Old Lady in Bernstein's *Candide* at the Old Vic, as Nettie Fowler in *Carousel* at the National Theatre.

In 1999 I was cast as Fezziwig in *A Christmas Carol* at the Chichester Festival Theatre, for my favourite director Sean Holmes. Pat invited me to stay with her for the full seven weeks of the run. I accepted her offer – but for the nights before matinée days only, as I enjoyed the late drive home to London after evening shows. Gosh we had fun! We drank wine, we ate delicious finger food, we talked and laughed and sang, to my accompaniment on the spoons. And the following morning Pat would provide a wonderful breakfast, dishing up the best poached eggs ever.

We re-established our friendship, which has continued to this day. Thank you, Pat, for forty-seven years and counting.

The RSC Centenary Season

I WAS WORKING for the Royal Shakespeare Company in their 1975 centenary season, which included *Henry IV*, Parts One and Two, *Henry V* and John Ford's *Perkin Warbeck*, that hadn't been performed since 1745.

After a performance of *Henry V* on a Wednesday night I got a call from my agent, Peter Crouch.

'Hello darling!'

'Hello Peter, lovely to hear you.'

'I've got an interview for you at 9am tomorrow morning at 20th Century Fox in Soho Square.'

'Gosh, I've got a matinée tomorrow.'

'That's why I made it 9 o'clock – to give you time to get back. You are seeing the guy who directed *American Graffiti*. I think he saw you as the Boy in *Henry V*.'

You could park on a meter in Soho Square in those days, so I did just that and a little before 9am went

With Barrie Rutter in *Henry V*, RSC, 1975.

through the portals of 20th Century Fox. I was met by a casting lady sitting behind a large desk. As I said my name, I noticed a small man scuttle through another door. I waited for what seemed like an age.

'OK, he'll see you now.'

I walked into the next room and there was a man laying a new carpet – bang, bang. 'Don't mind me.'

The director was sitting behind another large desk and was staring fixedly at its empty surface.

'This film is a cross between *2001: A Space Odyssey* and *The Four Musketeers*.'

I laughed.

'You think it's funny?' he said.

'Well, it does sound amusing.'

'How is your American accent?'

'Good for an Englishman,' I replied.

'Well, we'll probably dub you anyway.'

I thanked him and left to drive back to Stratford-upon-Avon. I heard nothing for several days, which usually means no. And then my agent rang: 'Hello darling. You didn't get Luke Skywalker but they've offered you a gold robot. I've turned it down.'

'Oh.'

'Well it could be anyone, darling – they won't even see your face.'

'What were the terms?'

'£100 a week for five weeks. Oh, and ½ per cent of the profits.'

To put things in perspective I was being paid £50 a week at Stratford, £60 when we transferred to the Aldwych in London. And $600 a week when we played at the Brooklyn Academy of Music in New York. We had to pay our own accommodation and living allowance out of that. There was no contest – I agreed with Peter Crouch that I should turn it down, and went to New York with the company.

When I got back from New York, Peter said, '*Star Wars* have been on again. This time the offer is to dub the first film and then play C-3PO in *The Empire Strikes Back*.'

'I can't do that to the actor who's playing it, Peter.'

So I turned it down again, and did a tour of a French farce called *Some of my Best Friends are Husbands*.

Kate Nicholls and I had bought a small house in Clapham and were expecting our first child. Friends persuaded us to get married, so we went along to Chelsea Register Office during the run of the farce. Our son Rufus was born on 9 September 1975.

The rest of my work that year was a film called *Stand Up Virgin Soldiers* and the BBC *Nicholas Nickleby*, in which Kate played Kate, I played Smike and Nigel Havers played Nicholas (Patricia Routledge was Mrs Mantalini). So a busy but normal year for a working actor – total earnings around £10,000, the same price as the house.

Don't ask what my ½ percent would have been worth from the *Star Wars* films.

While I was on tour in New York, Pat Routledge was also in town, with a musical called *1600 Pennsylvania Avenue*. It was, as the address suggests, about the Presidents and First Ladies of the White House. Pat was playing, hilariously, all the First Ladies. The music was by Leonard Bernstein and the book and lyrics by Alan Jay Lerner. It was backed by money from Coca Cola. On the opening night, Pat had asked me to be her 'plus one' at Sardi's. I raced back from Brooklyn in great excitement to sit with her at the top table.

When I had seen a preview of the show, Pat got a standing ovation for one First Lady taking over from another, which was managed in a song and aided by a hinged wig. Flicked forward it was curls, flicked back it was a bun.

The food was wonderful, drinks flowed, conversation glittered, and then, at about 2.30am the Maître d' stood on a chair and said, 'This is the *New York Times* review for *1600 Pennsylvania Avenue*. It reads like this…'

He paused and put it down.

'The *New York Post* review…'

By the time he had put that one down unread, the tables began to be cleared, and shortly afterwards the cast and crew assembled on the pavement outside as a light rain started to fall. Bernstein turned to Alan Jay Lerner and said, 'Well, I don't think we managed it this time. Shall we share a cab?'

I escorted Pat back to her suite at the Hampshire House on Central Park, where the fake antiques had fake woodworm. The show came off two days later.

I flew home at the end of our New York season and joined the tour of *Some of my Best Friends are Husbands*. It then came to the Mermaid Theatre at Puddle Dock in London, the brainchild and life's work of the actor-manager Bernard Miles. Bernard ran the theatre with no subsidy. He told me that he funded the shows from the beer sales at the longest bar in the city, the front-of-house bar, and used to stand in front of the theatre shouting into a megaphone: 'The welcome is warm – the beer is cold!' The pantomime was the same every year, *Treasure Island*, with Bernard himself playing Long John Silver.

In 1976 his family and friends said, 'Bernard, you are brilliant as Long John Silver, and have been every year since you opened the Mermaid Theatre, but we all feel you should give way to a younger man. Maybe someone well known from the telly. How about Roy Marsden?' Bernard was not pleased, but agreed. Most importantly he also agreed that Roy would be able to use his, Bernard's, parrot.

They put a publicity man onto the production who was well known for his wacky ideas, getting a lot of coverage for very little outlay. His idea this time was to have a parrot audition, which led to fearsome competition. Eventually, Bernard's parrot was announced as the winner, and retained his role. The parrot's job, when perched on Long John Silver's shoulder, was to squawk when the treasure chest was opened: 'Pieces of eight! Pieces of eight!' Bernard invested a lot of time with the parrot between the dress rehearsal and the first night. As the treasure chest swung open, the parrot excitedly squawked: 'You should have seen Bernard Miles in the part! You should have seen Bernard Miles in the part!'

Busking For Arnold

DURING MY SECOND year of working at the Leeds Playhouse I was living in a three-bedroom end-of-terrace house in Harehills. The rent was £5 a week, on condition that I would move out within a week if the house, which was on the market, sold.

On Sundays I sanded the floors and painted – one chocolate brown wall in the sitting room, white everywhere else except for the attic bedroom, which was purple. I cleaned the chimney and lit fires – and joss-sticks of course. It was glorious, and I lived there with Jane Kruthoffer whose sister owned the house.

When people came to view the house I showed them round, somewhat half-heartedly. But then someone made an offer and I thought, 'No, they can't – this is *my* house! It was nothing before I moved in!' I made an appointment with my bank manager at the Harehills branch of NatWest. His name was Mr Webber.

'You wanted to see me?'

'Yes, I want to buy a house.'

'Really, Mr Bourke?'

He pressed a button on his intercom machine.

'Could you bring Mr Bourke's account in here, please? Now, how much is the house, Mr Bourke?'

'Two thousand, three hundred and thirty-seven pounds.'

'How much have you got in your account, Mr Bourke?'

All my RADA training came into play and I answered with all the confidence I could muster.

'Seven pounds. So I only need two thousand, three hundred and thirty.'

'How much can you repay a week?'

'Fifteen pounds.'

'How will you do that?'

'Well I am used to paying £5 a week and I will let out the other two bedrooms at £5 each.'

'Really, Mr Bourke?'

'Yes.'

'Well, I don't know why I'm doing this but all right.'

Gosh! I walked back to 2 Hovingham Mount, Harehills, Leeds and looked at the end wall. 'Don't you dare fall down!'

I was earning £25 a week at the Playhouse but I needed more money so the following Saturday I set up with a mate in the Merrion Centre at lunchtime to busk. Some guitar playing, a few songs, a bit of clowning – don't laugh, I am taking jumping over this matchbox very seriously – learning early on that you have to build to a proper finale and then pass round the hat.

All was going swimmingly, the cash was coming in, when a uniformed official came over and called a halt. 'You can't busk here – this is private property. You'll have to move on.' We started packing up. A dignified man in an astrakhan coat with a plummy voice asked us, 'What do you earn in an hour?' We carried on clearing up. 'Only my wife said, "Never pass a street busker without giving him money."' He had his hand inside his coat, reaching for his wallet. 'I don't know the answer to that,' I said, 'because we've been moved on as this is private property.' 'I know it's private property – I own it. I was wondering if we could come to some sort of arrangement.' We thought he was joking. 'We have to go,' I said.

So we stood outside the Merrion Centre and started our act again. Not long afterwards, with no money in the hat, the police arrived. We went back inside and found the man in the astrakhan coat, in his office.

'What sort of arrangement?'

'Well, actors pay agents 10 per cent. Why don't you play for an hour next Saturday then we can meet and count the money – think of it as renting space.'

This is the moment to tell you that the man turned out to be Arnold Ziff, who founded the property company Town Centre Securities, ran Stylo Shoes and was a chief magistrate in Leeds. Saturday took a long time coming but gave us the opportunity to polish our act. We played the lunch hour and made £10, which we counted out in the security guard's office, in front of the boss, and gave him £1.

I didn't busk again until 1979, and then it was under the awning of the Old Vic to raise funds for the theatre's renovation. My friend Sean Seymour and I raised a pound a minute on the first night of *King Lear* with Timothy West. Terry Hands, my old director at the RSC, was embarrassed that one of his actors was reduced to this. Trevor Nunn gave £10. Sean and I busked whenever we needed to, and for ourselves, after that.

My original choice of partner was not Sean, it was Jeremy Irons, but in the end he and I just had a single rehearsal – he wanted to play a one-stringed fiddle as a white-face clown, which wasn't quite the double-act I'd envisaged. Thinking of it now I realise it would probably have been brilliant but at the time it didn't seem to work.

I owe Jeremy a deep debt of gratitude. When Kate (Nicholls) and I came back from our son Rufus's funeral in Herefordshire two things happened: a cat ran into the house over a pile of letters on the doormat, and the telephone started to ring. I picked up the phone.

'Hello Peter, Jeremy here. Sinead's away and I'm

cooking supper for a couple of friends. Would you and Kate like to come? You can bring Rufus.'

'Jeremy, oh! Haven't you heard? Rufus died. It was a cot death. We're just back from his funeral. I'll ask Kate but we're not great company.'

'Listen, you should come. We'll eat and then I'll get rid of the others. I'll light a fire and we can talk.'

Kate and I agreed to go. We didn't have anything else to do.

It was a good decision. The other couple, primed I'm sure, left soon after 10. Jeremy built up the fire, we snuggled into the sofa and he gave us the space and all the time we needed to talk about Rufus.

We left as dawn broke and went back to our empty little house. Although we had put the cat out when we left she was there when we returned. And there she stayed, and there she delivered five kittens while we were watching the last episode of *The Mayor of Casterbridge* a year later. It was my best scene, a monologue over Henchard's (Alan Bates) dead body. Upstaged by kittens.

General Sir Brian & Lady Nancy Horrocks

I WAS SIXTEEN or seventeen when General Sir Brian and Lady Nancy Horrocks invited me and my parents to drinks. They were patients of my father's and lived in a long low Somerset farmhouse with stone flags, an inglenook fireplace, whitewashed walls, mullion windows and Nancy's artist's studio in a stone outhouse.

Brian was a great General who fought in both World Wars: 'Brian, Sir Brian, as bold as a lion.' Nancy was a lady in her own right, and a fine artist.

Nancy was late down to drinks – by the time she sat next to me on the sofa I had a Campari and soda in my hand. 'I hear you're going to be an actor,' Brian had said, 'in which case you should drink what they all drink at the BBC – Campari and soda.'

I had been told that Nancy was shy but her first words to me were: 'Have you read *Portnoy's*

Complaint?' I hadn't but knew what it was about. So I probably blushed and took a big swig of my Campari, a drink I didn't like but seemed to have nearly finished. 'I knew you'd like that,' said Sir Brian, taking my glass and refilling it. I wobbled out of their beautiful house feeling very grown up.

Sir Brian at the time had been doing a series of reconstructions of battles for the BBC using trays of sand. They were brilliant programmes and he was mesmerising, rather in the mould of David Attenborough with his wonderful voice, depth of knowledge, charm and charisma.

The evenings with the Horrockses when I visited

my parents in Shepton Mallet were always a highlight. In late 1975, Brian summoned me and my then wife, Kate Nicholls, to the farm. 'I have been asked to recommend an actor to play me in a film about Arnhem called *A Bridge Too Far*. I have been offered Michael York, Christopher Cazenove and Edward Fox. What do you think?'

'Edward Fox,' we both said, having recently seen him in the film of *The Day of the Jackal*.

Brian telephoned Richard Attenborough the following morning. I know that because he accidentally telephoned my London number first, asking for him. A few weeks later when Edward was cast, I had a call from Brian.

'You know that actor you suggested?'

'Yes, Edward Fox.'

'Yes, him. He wants to meet me.'

'Well he would – he wants to do you justice.'

'I won't have much to say to him. He's coming next Monday, and getting a taxi here for 2 o'clock. Any chance you could be passing with your mother's dogs at 2.20?'

It was not a question, it was an order.

At 2.20 on the dot I was passing with my mother's whippets. The door was opened by Brian – 'Oh, what a lovely surprise. Nancy is in the kitchen – she'll make you a cup of tea. I've got someone with me.' At 4pm I drove Edward to the station. Three great friendships were formed that day.

The last time that we all got together was a Sunday when Edward and I drove in his newly restored BMW to the Old School House in Singleton, plus hamper, to give Brian and Nancy a surprise lunch.

We were met by Brian's unmanageable Boxer dog, who had eaten the stuffing out of one of their more comfortable chairs. They were in a muddle, and a bit thrown by our visit, but Brian was particularly thrilled with the goodies, eating with the pleasure of a starving man. And they both warmed to our company.

Brian moved to a nursing home shortly after that, in Fishbourne, where I visited him with my wife Britt, shortly before he died. He had just eaten a mince pie and, ever charming and gallant, kissed Britt with sugar still on his lips.

Field Marshal Montgomery wrote his obituary, as Brian had prepared Monty's. When Brian was in Somerset he lived in West Pennard and Monty in Bruton. I don't believe there was any love lost between them but they respected one another and collaborated on their mutual obituaries, meeting occasionally to update them.

After Brian died, Nancy moved near her son-in-law, who lived on the Mall in Chiswick. I visited her regularly, taking an avocado, her favourite food.

Brian and Nancy were always comfortably off. After the Second World War he had been head-hunted by Bovis, the building firm, and asked to be on the board of directors and 'troubleshoot', travelling around the country by helicopter. On one occasion Brian was desperate for a pee and they touched down in a field to allow this to happen. As they took off again, the pilot with perfect timing said, 'That *was* a VIP.'

Brian would always make sure that he was briefed on the building site staff, particularly if he had met them before – their names, their children's names, their animals' names – before sitting down with them in the lunchbreak with his sandwiches to find out their grievances. A leader of men who led from the front, as we saw in Edward Fox's true-to-life portrayal of him in *A Bridge Too Far*.

He also had income from his television programmes and from his wonderful autobiography, *A Full Life*, but I remember him saying to me, 'It doesn't matter how much you have saved; when you are my age and can't work any more or earn any more, you know you've got to make it last.'

Which reminds me of a morning out riding with my prep school headmaster, who pointed his riding crop at a grand country house in the Quantock hills.

'Do you see that house, Bourke?'

'Yes, sir.'

'It's a grand house.'

'Yes it is, sir.'

'There's a salutary lesson there, Bourke.'

'Is there, sir?'

'The couple who lived there, Bourke, had no

children, and when they were both seventy they decided to sell that beautiful house and spend the money over the next ten years, travelling the world. They stayed in the best hotels, ate at the best restaurants – and this is the point, Bourke – when they got to be eighty their money ran out. They hadn't expected to live that long and they died penniless.'

Not the case for Brian and Nancy. Brian had a state funeral in Westminster Abbey, which I was able to attend during rehearsals for a television comedy pilot, being filmed, would you believe, at Chelsea Barracks – where Brian had lived when he was courting Nancy. In *A Full Life*, Brian said of meeting Nancy, 'She taught me what beauty was. Before I met Nancy I thought the Chelsea Barracks were beautiful.'

I so enjoyed my weekly visits to see Nancy. The first time I had been to the Mall at Chiswick was as a paying guest of the widow of A. P. Herbert, thanks to an introduction from Brian. I stayed at the top of Lady Herbert's house, in a flat where her husband used to write. On some mornings she used to send her butler to invite me to join her for breakfast, which he served in full morning dress, with white gloves. Lady Herbert's passion was chess, and Brian warned me against taking her on.

I was working on a play for the BBC. It was called *America America* and was about the Pilgrim Fathers sailing from England in the *Mayflower*. It was an experimental studio production set against a white screen and directed by Donald McWhinnie, who was well known for directing plays by Beckett and Pinter. At my audition he said, 'If you are represented by Peter Crouch then you are a good actor. Do you want the part?' I did – I was useless at auditions and even worse at doing readings because of my dyslexia. When I read the script I discovered that it required me to do a scene naked. It was a monologue delivered as a duologue, with me playing the voice of conscience in my head. Donald asked me if I would wear coloured contact lenses but never said anything about being naked. It was all very 70s. When I was called from my dressing-room to the set it was, 'Peter Bourke to the set please, and Peter's make-up artist. This is a closed set, this is a closed set.' I went in a dressing gown, which I took off, in the fortunately warm studio. What amazed me was the number of crew members who had jobs to do that involved coming on to the *Mayflower* set. It was a taste, I am sure, of what many actresses go through.

When the show was aired in 1975 I was at Stratford and missed it. In fact I've never seen it, although 12 million people did. I remember wondering how many years I would have to play 'Boy' in *Henry V* with the RSC to be seen by so many.

I had such happy times with and because of Brian and Nancy, meeting many exciting and interesting people through them. They had friends everywhere, two of whom, Tom and Marie Last, peppered my two years working in rep in Leeds with restaurant treats and Sunday lunches.

Alan Bates

ALAN BATES WAS the perfect actor. I met him on the set of *The Mayor of Casterbridge* for the BBC. Our director David Giles suggested we had a rehearsal at his house the night before filming in Corfe Castle. I played Abel Whittle to Alan's Michael Henchard, often described as the Fool to his Lear. At 6pm the following morning Henchard was dragging Whittle through the streets without his trousers on, making an example of him for turning up late to work. Not having my trousers on involved a cunning device from the wardrobe department – a jock strap adapted as a G-string. But what I hadn't allowed for was the fact that I had to climb onto a cart, which meant lifting my arms, which in turn meant that the nightshirt that had just covered my backside no longer did. 'You're very brave,' remarked Alan. And all I could think of was the scene in the film of *Women in Love*, where he wrestled naked with Oliver Reed in front of a blazing fire.

My daughter Poppy studied *The Mayor of Casterbridge* at school and they watched the video. She didn't let on that it was her father playing the village idiot.

Alan was quite simply a joy to work with; the most giving actor, with a quality of listening. We had eighteen scenes together, culminating in the final scene of all: Abel Whittle making a speech over Henchard's dead body to Henchard's daughter. Alan was there for the establishing shot and I assumed that he would then leave, but no, he stayed for the whole of the filming, despite it being a Saturday and his twin boys' ninth birthday. David Giles, Janet Maw – playing the daughter – and I tried to persuade him to leave, but he said, 'I'll be there for the cutting of the cake. In the meantime I'll do my job.' I have to say it was a tremendous help having him there.

I next met Alan in the Green Room bar at the National Theatre after a show. I had heard that he had been offered the role of Sir John Brute in *The Provok'd Wife*, directed by Peter Wood. I had been cast as Razor, Brute's valet, so I told him how excited I was that we might work together again.

'Did I not tell you? I can't ever work at the National.'

'Oh no, you didn't tell me. Why?'

'Well, before the new building was completed, Peter Hall asked me to play Hamlet and Tamburlaine to open the theatre. The opening was delayed and I met with Peter to discuss his plans – was he wanting to do *Hamlet* in modern dress? What were the cuts? We were having lunch and we'd got to the main course before any of these things came up. I was a bit worried that we were running out of time so I broached the subject. Peter gulped down his lunch then said, "I've had to give it to Albert [Finney]. I hope you understand." Then he looked at his watch, got up and went – leaving me with egg on my face, and the bill to pay, and friends to explain to. So you will understand why I can't work here, not under any circumstances.'

And I did understand. Looking back I am struck by the fact that no one is safe in our business. We are all commodities in the marketplace.

Nicky Henson

NICKY HENSON AND I met in a rehearsal room at the National Theatre in January 1980. Our director, Michael Rudman, introduced us: 'This is Nicky Henson, this is Peter Bourke. You two are going to get on famously.'

I looked at Nicky as he took off his motorcycle helmet and thought, 'I can't think what we will have in common.' Nicky was a 60s British film star, who had appeared in *Here We Go Round the Mulberry Bush*, *There's a Girl in my Soup* and *Witchfinder General*, as well as *The Bawdy Adventures of Tom Jones*, and many more. His credibility at that time came from his brilliant work at the Young Vic. All of us drama students saw and admired his work, and some modelled themselves on him. I think Robert Lindsay owes a lot to Nicky.

I had seen him do farce in *Rookery Nook*, high comedy in *Man and Superman* and star in musicals such as *Camelot* and *Canterbury Tales*. At the Leeds

Playhouse I had played the 'Nicky Henson parts' in *Canterbury Tales*. Big shoes to fill.

Nicky had glamorous, starry girlfriends. I thought him out of my league. Rehearsing *The Browning Version*, Nicky was playing opposite Geraldine McEwan, who I later discovered he had fancied for years, and who I knew as the wife of Hugh Cruttwell, our principal at RADA. We opened at the Sunderland Empire in a double bill with another Rattigan play, *Harlequinade*. I was travelling in and living out of my parents' camper van.

'Where are you parking?' asked Nicky.

'Down by the sea.'

'Why don't you park in the car park of my hotel, then you can use my shower and eat my breakfast. I don't eat breakfast.'

'Gosh, thank you.'

Nicky never ate breakfast but he was very keen on brunch, which when we toured to Baltimore some eighteen months later was frequently taken at stalls by the harbour. Curried goat was a favourite.

Our second date on the tour was the Norwich Theatre Royal, where we shared a dressing-room.

'You don't rush home at weekends,' Nicky said. 'Is everything all right with you and Kate?'

Nicky knew my first wife, Kate Nicholls, as she and Nicky's former girlfriend Susan Hampshire had played mother and daughter together in *The Pallisers*.

'Ah no, things aren't great. Kate's met someone else.'

'We should go out one night.'

And that was the start of our forty-year friendship. We had a second adolescence, with less acne and more pocket money. Such fun did we have that we made a pact not to fall in love with anyone for a year – and then extended it for another year. We were playing at the National Theatre in the Rattigan plays and *The Provok'd Wife*, an unfortunate Restoration comedy to be in if you are going through a divorce.

Our NT contracts ended after our tour to Baltimore. We decided to go up the coast when we finished and holiday with Tessa Dahl on Chappaquiddick Island. Tessa had recently married James Kelly, who she lived with in Boston and London but they spent summers on the island, where they had two glorious houses with access to the beach. Paradise.

We had agreed to have a night in New York on our way back to Baltimore. Nicky was terrified of New York – he had a friend there who had found a dead body in the lift, and he had heard various other horror stories. I had spent a short season there with the RSC and booked us a cheap and cheerful hotel that I had stayed in before on 49th and Broadway. When we checked in, the concierge led us to 'a special room, gentlemen'. This turned out to have a double bed, black gloss walls and mirrors on the ceiling. It was a bit of a moment. I fell over myself trying to explain, wondering if Nicky thought that all our previous clubbing and socialising escapades had been a sham.

Nearly forty years later, Nicky and I were working together on a French farce, *Bang Bang*, adapted by John Cleese from Feydeau's *Monsieur chasse!* Nicky was directing.

'You book the rooms, matey.'

I scoured the digs list and found a perfect-sounding flat in an old school that had a main bedroom with an open fire and a loft bedroom above the living area.

Nicky had a production meeting in Colchester and we agreed that we would drive up together early and check out the digs. Our landlady met us at the door; she didn't have long as she was giving a flying lesson.

'Here is the kitchen and here is the bedroom. The

open fire draws beautifully and I think you'll find the bed very comfortable.'

'I think you advertised another bedroom?'

'Yes, it's up a ladder out of the kitchen. But it's a single bed – I don't think anyone has ever used it.'

'I'm going to use it – that will be my bed.'

She looked surprised. Her determinedly broad-minded attitude towards two actors had been misplaced. Nicky got considerable mileage out of the tale of our viewing at the production meeting that followed.

But back to New York. After we had checked into the right room at the hotel, Nicky agreed to going on a visit to Tiffany's, followed by a gin sling on Fifth Avenue. It was a gentle walk past Central Park and to top it all off I had booked us a table at Sardi's, mentioning that we were two National Theatre actors in the hopes of getting a good spot. We didn't – our table was at the back by the loos, the food was cold when it arrived and we were largely ignored, which at least enabled Nicky to pocket one of the ashtrays. After a bit Nicky looked at his watch and said, 'I'll be back in a minute. I've promised to meet an old mate and bring him back here after his show.' I sat for a long twenty minutes before Nicky returned. As he came in with his old mate, the entire restaurant stood up and applauded. We were moved to a table in the middle of the room, champagne appeared in an ice bucket, our orders were replaced with warm food. It was Jim Dale, who had just won a Tony award for his performance in *Barnum* and was the toast of Broadway.

After a magical evening, Nicky and I rolled back to the hotel on 49th and Broadway, said our goodnights and were about to fall into bed when we heard a gunshot in the street, followed by two more. Within a very short space of time we were at Penn Station, catching, to quote Nicky, 'The first thing smoking' to Baltimore. And home.

Soon after we got back – Nicky to Brentford Dock and me to Brixton – Nicky said to me, 'I think we've become friends, don't you? I wasn't looking for more friends, I thought I had my quota, but you seem to have slipped through the net.' We renewed our pact not to fall in love with anyone for another year.

Early one morning I was in the make-up department at Granada Television in Manchester when the phone rang.

'There's a call for Peter Bourke.'

'What? At 6 o'clock in the morning? Who is it?'

'It's Nicky Henson.'

He came on the line.

'How on earth did you know to get me here?'

'You're in the studio today so you were bound to be in make-up at this time.'

'What's so urgent?'

'I want to break our contract.'

'What! Why?'

Marguerite Porter (© Antony Dufort).

'I met someone at a charity do last night at Liberty's. She's a ballet dancer called Marguerite Porter.'

I had only been to the ballet once, and that in the 60s with my mother and father, to see Margot Fonteyn and Rudolf Nureyev in *Romeo and Juliet*, so I didn't know who Marguerite was.

'It's Nicky Henson on the phone,' I explained to the make-up artists.

'Tell him to get up here,' they shouted as one. 'We love Nicky.'

'Did you hear that, Nicky? I don't think this is a good time to be breaking the contract. There are beautiful girls here.'

'It's too late.'

I told him I needed to meet Marguerite before releasing him from the contract, and arranged to go to London for the weekend.

We met in Jules wine bar and over a bottle of champagne I agreed that his contract could be terminated for this beautiful, Audrey Hepburn-lookalike ballerina.

Our friendship changed, of course – we met up to play snooker rather than to meet girls. Then in 1983, Nicky and Marguerite matched me up with Britt, and we would meet as couples, spending Christmases together in a house we used to rent in Dorset, and later at my place in Brixton or theirs in Fulham and then Kew; times that were always filled with fun and laughter.

Stories of Nicky Henson the actor and Nicky Henson the friend could fill two volumes. He was always interesting and always interested – but above all, he was funny. The last thing I said to him before he died was, 'We've had a lot of fun, haven't we?'

'We've had a lot of laughs,' he replied.

Nicky contracted cancer in 2000, at Christmas, and had 50 per cent of his stomach removed, and 40 per cent of his colon. My father, when he heard the diagnosis, said, 'There is no reason on this evidence that he shouldn't live into his seventies.' When Nicky was first ill he said, 'Listen, I am going to treat this as a job. And I've said to Marguerite that we must never feel sorry for ourselves.'

For the next nineteen years Nicky continued to do great work. He played the West End and Broadway in

Jumpers, which came off just in time for him to play in the film *Syriana*, with George Clooney. He also did a long stint in *EastEnders*, voiced video games and appeared in the film *We Still Kill the Old Way* with his great chum Ian Ogilvy. He always earned a good and steady living as a working actor.

What gave him the most pleasure latterly was working as a teacher and director at LAMDA, where he played a large part in securing funding for a new theatre. Friday nights he would take his students to the pub, buy them drinks and talk theatre. I would love to have been a fly on that pub wall.

A group of his students put on a play at the Red Lion pub in Islington called *The Play That Goes Wrong*. The rest, as they say, is history – it became a huge hit.

Nicky ended his days in Denville Hall, the 5-star old actors' home. I visited him once a week to take him into the town for shopping and for lunch, when we would reminisce, tell stories and laugh. He knew what he wanted to do from a very young age, remembering how he would sit at the top of the stairs, listening to his actor-manager father and his friends laughing and talking, breathing in the smell of cigar smoke. Craning forward to get a better view he slid all the way down the stairs, landing in a heap at the bottom.

'I meant to do that,' he said, as he picked himself up.

That probably stood him in good stead years later when he had to fall down stairs eight times a week in *Noises Off.* Nicky lived to make people laugh, as his father Leslie had before him.

One last anecdote about Nicky. When his father died, Nicky was at boarding school and learnt about his father's death from a newspaper article. The article said, 'He leaves a wife and one son.' Nicky was devastated, as he had a much older brother called Joe, who he idolised. When he next saw Joe he was a bit off with him and Joe asked him what was wrong.

'I thought you were my real brother and you're not.'

'Why do you say that?'

'Because it said so in the papers.'

'Ah,' said Joe. 'Did Mum never tell you? Dad had three marriages – the first was Gladys, the last was Mum, but throughout all his marriages, Mum was his mistress. I was born out of wedlock and you were born legitimately, but to the same mother. So we are natural brothers.'

Nicky and Joe looked just like their Dad, as does Joe's son Adam, who now runs the Cotswold Farm Park that his father started. The 'Adam's Farm' feature on *Countryfile* has made Adam a TV star, just like his uncle Nicky.

When Nicky died, Michael Rudman, who first introduced us back in 1980, dedicated his latest play to 'Nicky Henson, who taught me a lot about acting and friendship'. I couldn't put it better.

Ralph Richardson

Sir Ralph had a disastrous flop in the West End called *Alice's Boys*. As he had placed his faith in the play and turned out to be wrong he didn't trust his judgement so he rang Peter Hall at the National and said 'I'll come and work for you and play as cast.'

His dressing-room was next to mine – his to himself, mine in a row of cubicles in a long shared room – but as they were both on the corner of the central courtyard, if I looked out of my window I could see Ralph sitting, reading *Principia Mathematica*. He said he felt he ought to read it but admitted to never getting past page 5.

We all had to sign in at the stage door before 'the half' and I would shamelessly hang about, waiting for Ralph to arrive, at first on a motorbike and latterly in a gold-coloured Mercedes. He had a very camp dresser, said to be the model for Ronald Harwood's play *The Dresser*, who would also be hanging around, waiting to meet 'Sir' and escort

him to his dressing-room.

Invariably, Ralph would ask:

'Any Monday news today?' or 'Any Friday news today?'

'Ooh, Sir Ralph, you'll never guess...'

At which point, having distracted him with a question, Ralph would slip through any door available and hide.

Turning to me in consternation, his dresser would say, 'Have you seen Sir Ralph?'

I always pretended I hadn't. When he found him, usually under a desk, his dresser would say, 'You'll never guess who's in tonight?'

'Never mind that, who *isn't* in?'

If you engaged Ralph in conversation he would say, 'You must meet my friend Gordon – come and meet him after the show tonight.' If you were lucky enough to get that invitation you would knock on his door and say – 'You said to come and meet your friend Gordon, who's in tonight.'

'Ah yes, did I? Would you like him with tonic?'

He'd down his glass in one and say, 'Now for pleasure,' before sipping the next.

I was told a story about Ralph by my first father-in-law, Anthony Nicholls, which went like this: coming home early from rehearsal one day, he stood in the hallway and called out: 'Darling, I'm home.' No reply. 'Hello darling, are you up here?' he said as he climbed the stairs, only to find, when he went into the bedroom, his wife in bed with a man. Solemnly, he went into his dressing-room, found his Army revolver, filled it with bullets and came back into the bedroom as the gentleman caller climbed out of the window and down the wisteria. Ralph leant out of the window and fired a shot and then another, before closing the window and saying, 'My darling, I think we both need a gin and tonic.' Nothing more was ever said on the subject.

He had a unique way of solving disputes. On the first night of the first season of the National Theatre in the New Theatre on St Martin's Lane in 1963, Olivier and he tossed a coin to see if it should be

Richardson in *Cyrano de Bergerac* or Olivier in *Richard III*. Ralph won the toss, so when the NT took the two shows to Paris it was Olivier's turn.

Richard III had the most brilliant reception, with Olivier as Richard and Ralph as Bolingbroke. At the first night party Ralph was conspicuously absent – he had returned to his hotel, only to be woken by Olivier knocking on his door at two in the morning. 'Ralphy, we triumphed! *I* triumphed! That was one of my greatest nights in the theatre. Don't you agree?' Sir Ralph, who was a big man, opened the window, lifted Olivier up, turned him upside down and hung him out of the window by his heels, several floors up. He then returned him to an upright position saying, 'Good night, Larry.' Olivier is quoted as saying, 'I never understood why he did that.'

Ralph once told his son that he had something very important to tell him, a lesson in life. He got a primus stove and set it up in the drawing-room of his grand house in Regent's Park. Then he whisked up a couple of eggs and taught his son, nicknamed Smally, to cook an omelette. 'There,' he said, 'if you can do that you'll never starve.' Ralph loved omelettes and one day at the Savile Club, at 2.30pm, the head waiter said to him, 'Sir Ralph, the dining-room is about to close. Would you like to place an order?'

'Yes,' said Ralph. 'I would like a jam omelette.'

The waiter disappeared, soon to reappear.

'The chef has asked who the jam omelette is for.'

Harold Pinter (© Antony Dufort).

'Tell him it's for Sir Ralph Richardson.'

The waiter went off and came back again.

'The chef says no.'

'Who the hell do you need to be to get a jam omelette?!'

In rehearsal for Harold Pinter's *No Man's Land* he once asked, 'When does a pause become a silence?'

Pinter replied, 'After eight seconds.'

I saw Ralph in David Storey's *Early Days*, that was written for him, and he quite simply cast a spell over his audience at the beginning of the evening and took it off at the end. His last show at the National involved fireworks and when he died he left enough money for a rocket, known as Ralph's Rocket, to be fired at every first night (a custom that was finally stopped for 'health and safety reasons'). The rest of his money funded an actors' charity called the Ralph and Meriel Richardson Foundation.

With Miss Brighton and Peter Cook.

Roald Dahl

Roald Dahl's daughter Tessa and I were friends and, both of us being single parents, she allowed me on occasions to share the help of her daughter Sophie's nanny, Maureen. This was the start of a wonderful friendship between Sophie and my daughter Emily, still going strong today.

Tessa had an exciting circle of friends. Nights when I came offstage and went to pick Emily up from her house you never knew who you were going to meet: Miss Brighton and Peter Cook, for example (see opposite, photographed by another guest, our good friend Ingrid Seward). Peter Cook was a phenomenal wit, but so generous with it – he made everyone funny. He was infectious. You found yourself saying: "Did I *really* say that, I must try and remember it?"

On one such evening a 60s pop star offered me two lines of coke. "How much would that be on the open market?"

"About sixty quid."

At that time that was a weekend for two in Paris.

"I can't afford to like that" I replied. And remembered my father stating "Save drugs until you can't enjoy anything else."

One Sunday Roald invited Emily and me to lunch at Gipsy House in Buckinghamshire, where he lived. Sophie and her mother were coming too.

Roald poured a large gin and tonic and said to me, 'Come and see what I've got in my swimming pool.' I think I was expecting an alligator at the very least. Instead, when I entered the building that housed the pool, built with his gardener and friend Wally, what

I saw was a pool emptied of water and filled instead with a wonderful collection of 18th-century English furniture.

'That's a wonderful library table,' I ventured. 'And where did you get that kneehole desk?'

'I took a horsebox round France,' he said. 'All the best antiques stolen in this country end up in France.'

'Well, I don't think I've ever seen a better collection of 18th-century English furniture,' I said, after a pause.

'You know a lot about antiques, don't you?'

'Not really – only what I grew up with.'

'What are you doing at the moment?'

'I've just finished eighteen months' work at the National Theatre.'

Roald could not have been less interested.

'So you're out of work.'

'You could say that.'

'I'm setting up an antiques business for my son Theo.'

As a baby, Theo had been hit by a taxi in New York while being pushed in his pram and suffered terrible injuries. His life had been saved by Roald, who insisted that a hole be drilled in his head and a shunt inserted so that the fluid could be drained from his brain. This method is still used today and the shunt is named after him, the engineer Stanley Wade and the neuro-surgeon Kenneth Till – the Wade-Dahl-Till valve.

'I would like to offer you a partnership in the business,' Roald continued.

'But I don't have any money to invest – and I'm an actor who knows pretty much nothing about antiques.'

'You can learn – we can learn together. And acting's a mug's game.'

This from a man who was married to Patricia Neal, an Oscar-winning actress.

'Work with me and you will be driving a BMW within a year.'

'Well, that's a wonderful offer and I'd love to give you some time and help, but when the next good job comes along I'm off. So no name over the door.'

I worked with Theo and Roald for six months, sometimes staying at Gypsy House for nights at a time with Emily and Sophie. On one of those nights, when we had put the girls to bed, Roald told them a story about a big friendly giant who breathed dreams through the windows of little girls while they were asleep. They were primed.

When Roald knew they'd gone to sleep, I helped him put a ladder up to their bedroom window. Wearing a hat, wrapped up in a rug, lit from behind and clutching his mother's old ear trumpet, Roald climbed the ladder, rattled the bedroom window and breathed through the trumpet … The girls were beside themselves with excitement the following morning, telling us how they had been woken up by a big friendly giant breathing dreams through their window.

On another occasion Roald used weed-killer and a stick to write messages to the girls on the lawn.

He had a rigid and disciplined work routine. At 9am, after breakfast, he set off to the shed that he and Wally had built out of breezeblocks, taking with him a flask of coffee and a KitKat. He sat in an old armchair, placing a plank of wood across the arms to write on. Then he sharpened his pencil, got to work and there he remained until 12.30. When he came in, if I was staying I would follow him down to his wine cellar, which was full of bottles he had bought at auction. 'I have enough wine here to see me out,' he announced on my first visit. He would choose a wine and open it to let it breathe while he prepared a simple lunch. At 1pm he listened to the world news on the wireless, with a large G&T in his hand. At 1.15 we would all sit down to lunch at the long kitchen table, where many and various bars of chocolate were stacked up in the middle. Emily and Sophie were allowed to eat what they liked.

After lunch, at 2pm, Roald returned to his shed, where he stayed until 3.30 when he would come in and go upstairs to his bedroom, which was hung with Henry Moore pictures of sheep, and sleep till 4.45pm. Then it was back to the shed, this time sitting at a small table where he would type up the day's work on his old Army typewriter. Finally he would stack up the pages, weighing them down with his hip joint, removed in a hip replacement operation, as a paperweight.

When he reappeared in the house at 6pm, 'our' day began, usually with a game of snooker. Sometimes we formed a team against invited friends from Great Missenden. Roald was very competitive in everything he did, not just snooker, but also the growing of marrows, which he did with his friend Wally.

Roald's favourite poem, often quoted, was:

> My candle burns at both ends;
> It will not last the night;
> But ah, my foes, and oh, my friends—
> It gives a lovely light!

When I wasn't staying at Gypsy House he would call me from time to time and say, 'Let's meet in the Pimlico Road for supper, but first let's look in the antique shop windows and see what lighting and colours might work for Dahl and Son.' Roald's friend Felicity always joined us for supper – he had invested in her business, Carvers and Gilders, which had its home in Wandsworth. She lived in a large mansion flat on Prince of Wales Drive in Battersea, with her two daughters. Felicity later became Roald's second wife, and set up and managed the Dahl Foundation.

Roald taught me how to bid at auction: arrive late,

stand at the back, don't make a bid until the gavel is raised, then and only then, raise your arm, showing no intention of ever taking it down. The last auction we attended together was at Christie's and we were there to buy a pair of Chippendale library chairs. We were bidding against Malletts of Bond Street. Malletts' mark-up was 100 per cent; ours was 10 per cent, as Roald owned the shop and was using his own money. He had given me a cheque book to a £75,000 account and was at the time worth £17 million, being the largest living literary export England had. We bought the chairs for £4,000 – less than we were prepared to pay – and Roald took me for a lavish lunch in St James's.

Often Roald sent me and Theo on trips, especially to Stockbridge, equipped with a book of cheques signed by him. 'Buy what you think is good,' he'd say. The Dahl name worked on the dealers, who often took us back from the shops to their homes, to see prized things which sometimes we bought. It was serious fun and a real window onto Roald's world, and that of antique dealers. Our adviser was the well known dealer, John Bly of Tring, and when I returned to acting I did an episode of *Birds of a Feather* with him, both of us playing antiques experts – he to the manner born.

I was in the Alibi Club on the King's Road with Nicky Henson when he said, 'Bourke, you look like an out of work actor.'

'I have work, I'm an antique dealer.'

'Nonsense, you're an actor. Get a haircut and get a job, and you and I will open an antique shop when we're too old to act any more.'

I had a haircut, polished my shoes and went to audition for an old friend, David Carson, who had directed me in a dozen or so shows at the Leeds Playhouse. On the day of my audition I had a meeting with Roald.

'Where are you going today?'

'An audition for a telly series with Granada.'

'You really want this job, don't you?'

'Why do you say that?'

'You've polished your shoes. So, you're going back to acting.'

'Well, I always said I would.'

I left with Roald's blessing after six months of fun and friendship.

Alan Bennett

I MET PATRICIA Routledge in 1974. We were in a BBC Sunday afternoon adaptation of *David Copperfield* and we remained great friends after the series was finished.

Pat phoned me in 1984 and asked if I had ever been to Haworth.

'Why?'

'I've been asked to read *Wuthering Heights* for Cover to Cover Cassettes and I thought I should get onto those moors.'

Pat's father, a retired high-class gentleman's outfitter, was in hospital on the Isle of Man. Pat flew to see him regularly from Manchester airport so I arranged to pick her up on one of her return visits and drive her to Haworth in my VW Beetle. On our way, Pat said, 'I've invited Alan Bennett to join us for supper.'

'Will the restaurant at the B&B be good enough?'

'Oh yes!'

'Really?'

'He'll love it, whatever it's like. It will be copy for him.'

Alan arrived looking immaculate in his uniform of sports jacket, pullover, tie and grey flannels, with a present of mushrooms that he had picked near his cottage in Clapham (Yorkshire). We went into the bar, which, like the restaurant, was all wrought iron threaded with plastic vines. Pat was anxious about her father and went to call him from a payphone in the hall, with Alan and I summoning up all our combined wealth in coins and passing them to her. It took a long time to get through and check on her father (who turned out to be fine) and as the coins ran out, Alan said, 'This is Charlotte Brontë calling from a Haworth phone box. Will you accept the charge?' – a joke he recycled later in his brilliant documentary film about a hotel in Harrogate.

We ordered three sherries and were given a menu each.

'Oh,' said Alan, 'I know what I'll have – a Florida Cocktail. Oh no! I want White Bait, two words. I'll have that.'

It was a very funny evening, seen through the prism of Alan's take on it all. I asked him what he was working on.

'I don't quite know yet but it has something to do with pigs. My father was a pork butcher in Leeds during the War. It has something to do with that.'

He went on to say, 'No one should live with a writer. It's such a lonely job, and makes people impossible to live with. But I've had a good day today.'

Pat asked him to tell me about that lady he had living in a van in the parking space at the side of his house in Camden Town. Her van had broken down in Parkway, between Camden Town and Regent's Park. Alan had helped her by pushing the van while she, as he described, made elaborate hand signals and steered her van into his street. A few days later the police were trying unsuccessfully to move her on and Alan took pity on her. He suggested that she park, temporarily, in his parking space. Miss Shepherd ended up staying for fifteen years, pushing gradually at the boundaries he tried to impose until she had access to his downstairs loo and ran a flex from her van through a window to a plug in the house. Occasionally they had talks, and on one occasion she came up with a suggestion that she wanted Alan to pitch to BBC Radio, that she should be behind a curtain or a screen and answer questions from the public. As Alan said, 'On radio, it's not as if anyone would have known whether she was behind a screen or not.'

Changing the subject he suddenly said, 'Pat, I'm having an affair.'

'Alan,' she answered, 'I don't want to know.' It transpired that the affair was with his cleaner, a delightful hippy single mother.

I had heard from a member of the first cast of *Forty Years On* that at the end of the run one of the young cast members had asked Alan if he would back him to open a restaurant in New York. Alan did, and it was a great success.

Another thing I remember about that night in Haworth was Alan bemoaning the fact that 'playwrights who write comedy are never taken seriously.' The evening ended with a walk on the moors and the next morning we visited the Parsonage and the museum before returning to London.

When plans were being made to celebrate Harold Pinter's seventieth birthday, Alan was asked how he thought it should be marked. 'With a two-minute silence.'

He once found himself trapped by Ian McKellen at a concert for AIDS research.

'Alan, this is your chance to come out. Are you gay or not?'

'Asking me if I am gay is like asking a man who has been crawling through a desert whether he would prefer Perrier or Malvern water.'

Alan's diaries are such a good read, and a real insight into his thoughtful views. One of my great treasures is a card Alan sent me to wish me luck for his play *Single Spies* at Salisbury Rep. He signed it with a self-portrait sketch – a sketch he has developed as he has so often been mistaken for David Hockney and asked for his autograph. I like to imagine one of his drawings being identified as a Hockney self-portrait on the *Antiques Roadshow* in twenty years' time.

Robert Stephens

I DID A television series for Granada called *Studio*, about a recording studio in the middle of nowhere where bands stayed to record an album.

Richard Branson had one such place in Oxfordshire though his timing was unfortunate, as garage music was happening and no bands booked to stay. Richard went for so long without income that he let a friend stay for free, or rather for a percentage of whatever his output was while in residence. Six months went by and Richard asked Mike Oldfield what he was working on and for how much longer. It was *Tubular Bells* and it became the foundation of Richard's business fortune.

I was invited to join the *Studio* company by David Carson, who had directed me for two years in rep in Leeds and before that in finals at RADA. Included in the regular cast were Phil Davis, who I knew from the National Youth Theatre, Michael Feast and Robert Stephens, both of whom I knew by reputation. My

Maggie Smith, Robert Stephens and son Christopher.

mate Nicky Henson said, 'Great cast but it will never get made.' We were handsomely paid and most of us regulars stayed in some comfort. Robert stayed in the Piccadilly Hotel, which had an ornate blue and gold staircase leading up from the entrance hall and was the haunt of some very high-class women from what was then referred to as the oldest profession.

Robert was famous for his portrayal of Atahualpa in Peter Shaffer's *The Royal Hunt of the Sun* and for his marriage to Maggie Smith. Also for walking offstage in *The Double Dealer* at the National Theatre, leaving Ralph Richardson alone, unable to finish the scene and calling for the curtain to fall. Robert was discovered front-of-house, in full costume, propping up the bar, as the audience filed out for an early and unplanned interval. The director Michael Halifax dealt with the situation swiftly – the understudy, who had been playing cards, was thrown into Robert's costume and sent on stage to play the scene with Sir Ralph as the curtain rose again.

Robert went missing for several days. When he was due to come back, Peter Hall went around the *Double Dealer* company saying, 'We have Robert back and we must be extra nice to him. He is a genius and very sensitive.' To which an actor replied, 'Do us all a favour and sack him. He is an unprofessional drunk.' Robert was reinstated.

When we did our four months together on *Studio* there was a special offer on the trains from London to Manchester. An 8am train got us to rehearsals on time and we commuted together regularly. We sat near the buffet car and Robert would go off for coffee, bringing one back for me but never having anything himself. He never let me buy the coffee and eventually I twigged that he was having a stiff drink at the counter. One morning I said, 'Robert, I'm getting the drinks today. What would you like? A vodka and orange? Something else?'

'Good god, no.'

And so the charade continued.

Before *Studio* was aired we were all signed up for a second series, a series we were paid for but which never happened.

When Robert played King Lear at Stratford he received wonderful notices. Friends in the cast said, 'He's amazing, constantly inventive, and he's not drinking.' When I went to Stratford he suggested that we meet in the Arden, opposite the theatre. He joined me there and I asked him what he would like to drink. 'Nothing,' replied Robert, reaching behind a menu on the bar for a glass of clear liquid…

His King Lear was a thing of legend and he had the guts to sustain it. He received a knighthood for services to the theatre and he had the interesting idea of asking Prince Charles if he would like to work with him on speeches of Shakespeare's princes, as he would have an inside understanding of their role.

In the months we worked together Robert told endless stories – Maggie this, Larry that – but, whether at 7.45pm or 3am, he never once repeated himself.

Robert died on 12 November 1995 of liver failure, aged sixty-four.

Gilbert O'Sullivan

GRAHAM SINCLAIR, A friend from National Youth Theatre days, who I had recently worked with in a production of *The Merry Wives of Windsor* at Chichester, called me up to say that he was workshopping a show. He was writing and directing, it was called *Every Song Has Its Play*, starring and featuring the music of Gilbert O'Sullivan. It was the story of his relationship with his manager, Gordon Mills. Would I play Gordon Mills, and generally help out?

It was an extraordinary experience – rehearsing a show about someone's life with that person in the same room.

Gordon Mills, who already represented Tom Jones and Engelbert Humperdinck, discovered Ray O'Sullivan, persuaded him to change his name to Gilbert and gave him a cap to wear that shaped his image. In 1969 he asked Ray what he needed to live on and Ray said, '£10 a week'. He managed a little

With Penelope Keith and cast in *The Merry Wives of Windsor*, Chichester 1990.

more than that. Gordon became like a father to Ray and 'Clair', one of his early hits, was about Gordon's daughter, who Ray used to babysit.

Ray was very shy and in 1972, when he was the top recording artist in the world, he played Madison Square Garden in New York. He literally ran on, did his set, ran off and went back to his hotel.

In the late 70s he realised that he had made a lot of money but not seen much of it. He went to see a lawyer, who said that the contract he had signed when he was a teenager, so young that it also had to have his mother's signature, had given the rights of all his songs to Gordon Mills. The lawyer thought that the contract had a good chance of being thrown over in court but the court case was made doubly difficult as Ray's wife Aase's twin sister was Gordon's girlfriend at the time.

The court ruled in Ray's favour and he was returned the rights, along with a several-million-pound settlement. Gordon Mills died of a heart attack shortly afterwards. The court case inspired Elton John, Sting and many others to fight for the rights to their songs by taking their managers to court, often using Ray's lawyers.

We rehearsed in Battersea Arts Centre. One lunchtime Ray had a visit from a friend who had just bought the office block in Vauxhall that had Jeffrey Archer as a tenant on the top floor. He had bought it with his share of the writing credit of 'Congratulations' for Cliff Richard. There was a lot of money in pop music in the 60s and 70s.

We did a tour of one-night stands for *Every Song Has Its Play*, travelling to twenty-six venues in a tour bus previously used by Whitney Houston. Very rock and roll. In the year we toured, 'Alone again, naturally' was requested over four million times – it had become a gay anthem. I asked Laurie Holloway, our music director, what Ray would earn per play.

'Guess.'

'£10 per play?'

'A great deal more than that. He wrote it, he plays it, he sings it, he owns it now, and shares it with nobody.'

£40 million for one song in one year, I thought

Ray – Gilbert – O'Sullivan.

– sounds good to me. No wonder so many others followed Ray's example and took their managers to court.

Ray's wife Aase and their two delightful daughters came to our last performance. Until that night the girls hadn't known what their dad did for a living. They all lived in a mansion in Jersey that our director said, 'made JR's house in *Dallas* look like a semi'. My last contact with the family was in a former embassy in Oslo that Ray had bought Aase for her 50th birthday! Ray had a huge fan base – the show sold out everywhere and Gilbert O'Sullivan stayed behind after each one to sign autographs and pose for photographs.

Michael Denison & Dulcie Gray

Michael and Dulcie met at the Webber Douglas drama school. Dulcie was already a big star in films and he was a dashing Old Harrovian whose English teacher had been Terence Rattigan.

Michael's mother and father had died when he was very young and he grew up with his uncle in Ilkley in Yorkshire. His uncle was a bachelor who sent him to boarding school.

Dulcie grew up in India, with a nanny. She told me that she remembered her nanny getting her ready in her best dress and announcing, 'You are in your best dress and you must be on your best behaviour. Today you are going to meet your mother.' She was four years old.

Against everyone's advice, Michael and Dulcie married. He was nineteen and she was eighteen. It was a great and lasting love affair and they made

every effort possible to work together. They were keen on touring and travelled in style, driving either a Jaguar or a Rolls-Royce. They were often invited to stay with local dignitaries and their joint names on the bill guaranteed audiences.

And they were tremendous fun to work with. I had that treat twice. The first, *Tartuffe*, starring Leonard Rossiter, was not a happy rehearsal period as Leonard took against the director, Peter Coe, and against Michael, who was playing Orgon. During rehearsal Leonard realised that this was the better part. It was a very starry cast, with the only unknown a young actor playing his first professional role in England. When my best friend Nicky Henson came to see the show, he asked me,

'Who's that young kid?'

'Do you mean Richard E. Grant?'

'Yes, him.'

'Did you think he was good?'

'You and I could retire on him, son!'

At the first run-through of the play and before the director gave notes, Leonard walked out. Peter Coe chased after him, unsuccessfully, and came back into the rehearsal room saying, 'We've lost Leonard. Does anyone have Alec McCowen's number?' I had worked with Alec at the National Theatre in two plays and did have his number but kept quiet.

There were a number of things that Leonard was unhappy about and that night he spoke to our producer, Nick Salmon, who – as we discovered the following morning – persuaded Leonard to stay and to take over the directing of the play. When Leonard took the reins the first thing he did was to cut a lot of lines, especially from Michael's role of Orgon. *Tartuffe* is a great play and the role of Tartuffe is a star turn but Orgon can clean up. Leonard had become a star, in middle age, in the late 60s, when he played Brecht's Arturo Ui. He was a brilliant performer, but a complicated man.

Michael and Dulcie invited cast members to their wonderful home, Shardeloes, near Amersham, an Adam house built in the Palladian style. They lived in a flat there, with their three corgis, but what a flat! They retained the library, a bedroom, drawing-room, dining-room and sitting-room, maids' quarters, a spare room, bathroom and kitchen. The two main rooms were stunning, with furniture to match, and both led onto the garden. They lived as I imagined actors lived when I first joined the business. There was a man who had been a butler at the house before it was divided into flats and he would 'buttle' for their parties. This particular gathering was a lunch party, dubbed 'the wake', and Leonard was conspicuous by his absence.

The second chance I had to work with them came in the late 80s and was the national tour of Ayckbourn's *Bedroom Farce*. It was a hilariously funny play and Michael and Dulcie played an older couple, with a wonderful scene sitting up in bed together eating pilchards. Dulcie had the glorious line: 'My mother always used to say, "When sex rears its ugly head, close your eyes before you see the rest of it."'

They were on top form, loving touring, staying with friends and travelling in a splendid Jag. Altogether a much happier job, and the tour was extended from twelve to fourteen weeks.

While we were playing the Leeds Grand I was staying with my dear friends the Lasts in Ilkley, who suggested that I invite Michael and Dulcie to lunch at their beautiful house on the edge of the moors. They accepted and after lunch we visited some of the places Michael remembered from his childhood, growing up and spending school holidays in the area. Bolton Abbey was a highlight.

Dulcie visited me at Chichester Festival Theatre in 1998 and we lunched in the theatre restaurant. She told me that Michael had been unwell on a morning when she had promised to give a talk at a drama school. She said to him, 'I'll ring and cancel – they'll understand.' He insisted that she should go, so she did, and when she returned home later, she was met by Michael, wearing his dinner jacket and carrying an ice bucket with a bottle of champagne. They dined in style and reminisced about their years of marriage and theatrical partnership. Then they went to bed in their big four-poster.

Every night before going to sleep Dulcie would ask if their dog could sleep on the bed. And every night the answer was no. But that night the dog joined them and slept between them. When Dulcie woke in the morning, Michael was dead.

When I asked Dulcie how she was managing she said, 'I talk to him as if he was there. After nearly sixty years of marriage I know what his answers are. And I work. I don't need paying – I just need a driver, and my touring expenses covered.'

She told me that she was sixty-nine and Michael seventy-five when we worked together, and that she had been eighteen and Michael nineteen when they married. 'But…?' I said. 'Ssh,' she answered, 'If anyone thought I was seventy I'd never work again.'

Terry Donovan & Nobby Clark

Terry Donovan was a 60s – and 70s and 80s – photographer, a contemporary of David Bailey. He took the most brilliant photographs of women, especially actresses.

Nobby Clark was my favourite. He specialised in photographs in performance – ballet, rock and roll, and especially plays. He could make any play look like high art by his photography, but also took definitive portrait photographs of Bob Hoskins, Mick Jagger and Samuel Beckett.

When Beckett was rehearsing Billy Whitelaw in *Not I* at the Royal Court Theatre, Nobby was asked to photograph him in the lunchbreak. Nobby arrived early and sat in the stalls but Beckett noticed him.

'I'm sorry Billy, but Nobby Clark is here to take my photograph. We had better finish there.'

Nobby Clark.

'Before you go,' said Billy, 'What did you mean when you wrote this?'

'I haven't the slightest idea. Does that help at all?'

I got Nobby to do the front-of-house photographs for *Endgame* when I actor-managed it. We had a photo call for the press at the Battersea Arts Centre. They all arrived, with cameras, lights, shutters clicking, putting us through our paces. But no Nobby Clark. The press photographers were long gone and the cast members were having tea, out of costume, when Nobby arrived, a little the worse for wear and apparently without a camera.

I had known Nobby since National Youth Theatre days when he was the NYT's photographer. I don't think he ever got paid, even though he was then and still is the best in the business.

'Sorry I'm late. I had a night shoot in Liverpool.'

'Have you had any sleep?'

'Not yet.'

'Do you want a cup of coffee?'

'Better just get on.'

I coaxed the cast back into their costumes, saying 'This man is a genius.'

'OK, but he doesn't seem to have a camera.'

'Ah yes,' I thought, 'I am a bit concerned about that.'

But assemble we did, and Nobby unzipped his leather jacket and whipped out a Leica. He took eight photographs, processed them overnight and got them to me the following day. It was his brilliant and powerful photographs that accompanied all the national reviews. I will always be grateful to Nobby for those photographs, especially the huge one that went onto the canopy at the Arts Theatre, surrounded by lights.

Terry Donovan I met when he had bought the rights to film the National Theatre's production of Tom Stoppard's *On the Razzle*. We were rehearsing at the Old Vic, where we met for a 'walk through' before lunch, which Terry announced would be provided in the Green Room. I had never seen a spread like it. He had shares in a catering company, who had laid it all on, accompanied by champagne.

'Gosh, this is kind,' I said.

'Not at all – it's an economy.'

'How so?'

'Well, if people go out to lunch and come back late they're wasting everyone's time and money. This is peanuts compared to that. Make it really good and everyone stays in the building.'

I was reminded of being late in my first job in Leeds and John Harrison, our director, saying 'You are two and a half hours late.'

'Ten minutes,' I said apologetically.

'Multiply the minutes by the number of people here and that is the time you have wasted.' I was never late again, except once…

In 1975 I'd had afternoon tea in London with my new friend Patricia Routledge before heading back to Stratford-upon-Avon. I left Pat at 4pm for the 7.30 show in Stratford. Ten minutes later I was on the West Way, where I remained for one and a half hours. At a quarter to six I got free, having chewed the steering wheel of my VW Beetle in frustration. I had one hour and 45 minutes till curtain up, for *Henry IV*, Part Two, in which we all took a line here and there of the opening speech. 'Open your ears, for which of you will stop the vent of hearing when loud Rumour speaks.'

I found a phone box, wasting valuable time, and

rang Michael Hyatt, our company manager, to explain, saying that I would make the performance, but only just – and could a dresser have a cloak ready to cover my day clothes. I would get into costume later. Back into the Beetle and my foot on the gas. We all had understudies but none of them would know which line to deliver in that opening Prologue. I got there eventually, and was even first on stage, changing in the wings.

That was a lesson learnt – always leave at least twice the amount of time you think you need.

When rehearsals finished on day one of *On the Razzle*, Terry thanked us for our hard work and said, 'If you phone your agents you will find that half of your fee has already been paid.' He held that people work better when they know they are valued. We continued in this perfect working environment all through filming – never rushed and always respected. And then we ran out of time! The stage crew came on stage and called a halt to proceedings with two scenes still to film.

'That's it,' said the head of the stage crew.

'Cast,' said Terry, 'will you work overtime?'

'Of course,' we said in unison.

'I will come and talk to you all in a minute,' said Terry, and he walked offstage.

I followed him, saying, 'They wield a lot of power here. Their strike postponed the opening of the building.'

'Listen, son,' said Terry, 'I was born on the Mile End Road, I know these people.'

I followed him to the stage door, where his Rolls-Royce was parked. He opened the boot and got out a briefcase. We went and found the stage crew. Terry opened his briefcase and took out bundles of notes.

'I know you have your rights,' he said, 'but does that help?' He handed each crew member a stack of notes, giving the head of the crew the rest of the money in the briefcase saying, 'Keep it.'

We all went back to work.

'I hope you're not out of pocket,' I ventured.

'Well, I sold this film here and to the States for double what it cost, so it's all fine.'

And fine it was. As we finished filming, the second half of our fees was biked to our agents. Such style. Old school.

Now everyone takes photos on their phones but back then it was an artform, and both Terry and Nobby were the best exponents of that form.

Ed Mirvish

I PLAYED STREAKY Bacon in David Hare's *Racing Demon* in Chichester, where it was picked up by Ed Mirvish, the Canadian producer, who with his son David bought the Old Vic theatre and poured millions of pounds into refurbishing it.

He had two theatres in Toronto, one that he built to house the big shows like *Miss Saigon* and called the Princess Diana. The one we played in was called the Princess Alexandra – and he had bought it to save it from being pulled down and the site turned into a car park. As he said, 'Once I'd bought it I had to produce shows.'

Christopher Morahan had directed *Racing Demon* at Chichester but couldn't stay beyond the technical rehearsal because of other commitments so had employed a young director called Sean Holmes to see the show into the theatre. After the dress rehearsal, Sean said to Mark Kingston, John Harding and me, 'I'd like to have a look at the Church House scene – I

think we might be missing a trick there.' We looked at each other, and a bit of eyebrow-raising went on. Then we got up and rehearsed the scene and it came to life. 'He's good,' we muttered in the wings. That night in the pub I asked Sean if he would re-direct *The Suitcase Kid* for me for its transfer to the Tricycle Theatre and offered him £1,000 with the option to play pool for £100 a game to give him the chance to get his money up (and me the chance to save a bit). Fortunately for this actor-manager, although Sean is a brilliant director he is less good at pool. The things we do to balance the books. I take comfort in the fact that his excellent production led to more good work for him at the Tricycle with *The Price*, with Warren Mitchell, transferring to the West End.

Ed had started his business quite literally on an orange box, having cashed in his wife's life insurance, buying some sportswear and selling it from a box on the street. The business grew until he was able to open a department store called Honest Ed's – it's in *The Guinness Book of Records* for having the most lightbulbs on the outside of a building. At Honest Ed's there was always a 'door opener' – say a mink coat for $100 – but once inside there was everything from a dentist to someone to help with immigration papers, plus a post office and all manner of things to buy at knock-down prices. It was not unlike TK Maxx today – he was way ahead of his time. His wife was a sculptor and when he'd made his millions, Ed built Mirvish Village – affordable housing and studios for artists – in her honour. And very beautiful it is.

Ed bought warehouses and turned them into huge restaurants, all themed – Ed's Chinese, Ed's Roast Beef, Ed's Indian. These vast places had appropriate furniture and décor, and everything was for sale. When he brought *Racing Demon* to Toronto he'd buy us dinner every night after the show in one of these restaurants. They were always full and everyone there seemed to know him.

I sat near Ed whenever I could and hung on his every word. 'I didn't plan to be a theatre producer,' he said, 'but once I'd bought the Alexandra there was no going back. Actually, at the Old Vic I was more of a benefactor than a producer.'

He sold the theatre eight years later for £8.5

million – I hope he got his money back. What he did get, that money can't buy, was an honour from the Queen, 'The closest thing to a knighthood that a Canadian like me can get from Her Majesty.'

I told him that I had bought his biography and was loving it. 'Yes, well, they asked me to co-operate with my biographer and I said "I don't remember a thing," but when they told me what they were planning to pay me I remembered everything!'

Jacqueline Wilson

My daughter Poppy was given a book called *The Suitcase Kid* for her tenth birthday and we started reading it together in our house in France, taking a few lines each. It was Poppy who said, 'This would make a great play, Daddy.' I set about getting the rights and asked Jacqueline if she would adapt it for the stage.

I still have her excellent first draft, which received a rehearsed reading at the Battersea Arts Centre. I sent it to Alan Ayckbourn, who writes brilliantly for children. He said he thought he could help, if Jacqueline would be happy to meet with him in his home town of Scarborough to discuss. Sadly that meeting never took place so with Jackie's approval I got a friend, the playwright Sam Snape, to adapt it.

I took a six-month lease on The Brix, a theatre built with funds from the GLC in the roof of St Matthew's Church in Brixton. It had 337 seats and a beautiful stained glass window as a backdrop.

It was 1997 and the time of A4E – Arts for Everyone. I was confident that the project would tick all the boxes. I was told to 'proceed as if you have got the grant' and that they were sure it would work out. I applied for funding to Lambeth Council, as the project was aimed at primary school children and the ILEA, who used to fund school trips for children, no longer did so. Lambeth turned me down. I asked to see them so that they could explain what their department funded and how I could tailor the show to meet their criteria. Then I applied again.

By now I was realising that the only way I could be sure of raising the money was to sell tickets. I got a list of thirty-seven schools in the area and sent the heads and drama teachers a letter announcing *The Suitcase Kid* at The Brix. I followed up the letters with countless calls and finally every school booked about 100 seats. The price ranged from £50 to £200 a school and there was one that couldn't afford a penny so I agreed that they could come for free.

The Council turned me down again. I told the Council that I would alert the South London press, picket the town hall and let everyone know why I'd had to cancel the project.

'You and a handful of children outside the town hall don't frighten us.'

'I have thirty-seven schools booked and approximately 3,700 children. I'm sure we can cover the length and breadth of the building. And I'm only asking for £3,000 to cover the shortfall.'

Within three hours I got a call from the National Westminster Bank in Brixton to say that there was £3,000 in my Brix account.

Children walked from their schools, in the snow on occasion, to see a show about a child from a broken home and learning how to cope with the situation, with the help of Radish the toy rabbit.

I liked Jacqueline Wilson, and the way she addresses so many difficult issues in her beautifully written books. In the brief time I knew her I met both her husband and her daughter. Bob Wilson had asked that his last posting as Chief Constable be in Brixton, before he retired to work with the Citizens' Advice Bureau. We who live in Brixton owe Bob a great debt of gratitude, for it was he who, after the riots, invited Lord Scarman to Brixton to meet prominent members of the West Indian community before he wrote his report and recommendations. Bob instigated the Brixton Challenge regeneration scheme and hosted Nelson Mandela and Prince Charles at the newly built recreation centre.

So it was particularly poignant to perform *The Suitcase Kid* at St Matthew's and I still treasure the review in *The Independent*: 'An adult show for kids'. We transferred the production to the Tricycle Theatre in Kilburn, run by Nicholas Kent. Two new actors were cast as two of the original cast had gone on to other jobs, and the production was directed by Sean Holmes. It sold out but with the cast change and a new director we needed more rehearsal and the costs went up. Nick Kent and I agreed to fund the extra costs and to put on more performances – which also sold out. So quickly did the tickets sell that Jacqueline's new agent couldn't get tickets for three BBC producers who wanted to come. Unfortunately they did manage to get in somehow because when I was offered a fourteen-week tour by a big West End management it wasn't possible – the rights had been sold to the BBC.

Barrie Rutter

BARRIE AND I became friends when we were both at the National Youth Theatre in the 60s. He was another great old-school actor-manager, perhaps the last. He started his own company, Northern Broadsides, in 1992, after the Tony Harrison play he was appearing in, *The Trackers of Oxyrhynchus*, was judged too expensive to tour. Barrie's assessment was that the administration costs were too heavy and with the help of some of the *Trackers* cast the company was formed.

He was a great motivator – when he asked you to do something it was more of an order than a request. All of us who had been members of the National Youth Theatre felt a great loyalty to its founder, Michael Croft. While I was there, Barrie asked me to do a turn for a fundraiser for the Shaw Theatre, that was to become the NYT's permanent home.

One Friday I was cast to start work on the Monday for the RSC's 1975 centenary season. I ran nervously

up the stairs to the rehearsal room in Floral Street, Covent Garden when who should come past me but Barrie.

'Ay oop, wanker, what the fuck are you doing here?'

He summed up my thoughts and was strangely comforting.

When in the coffee break he approached me and another NYT actor, Gareth Armstrong, it was to say: 'Bourkie, you, me and Gareth, we should get digs together. We can have a few bevvies, fuck a few birds, it'll be great.'

Gareth interjected: 'Barrie, if we are going to share digs there's something you need to know about me.'

'You're what? You're fucking what? Oh well, we'll have a few bevvies anyway.'

I excused myself as I already had digs arranged, and my girlfriend Kate to share them with. Shortly after this, Gareth met his life partner, a market gardener. On the morning after their first night together, in those shared digs, Barrie brought them breakfast in bed.

I was touring in *Bedroom Farce* some years later, with Michael Denison and Dulcie Gray. We were playing the Leeds Grand and I went to have a look at the newly built West Yorkshire Playhouse, now renamed the Leeds Playhouse. I had spent my first two years out of drama school at the old Leeds Playhouse and turned up feeling nervous, and a bit of an imposter. Who should be standing in the front-of-house café but Barrie Rutter.

'Ay oop, wanker, what the fuck are you doing here?'

'I'm on tour with a play at the Grand.'

'You're working?'

'Yes.'

'You can buy me tea.'

'Happy to. What are you up to?'

He told me how *Trackers* had been too expensive to tour to America – 'too many bloody administrators to pay' – and that he'd set up a tour of England with *Richard III.*

'What theatres are you playing?'

'We're not playing theatres, we're playing sports halls, swimming baths, carpet warehouses.'

'Who's going to play Richard III?'

'Fuck off. I've set it up, raised the money, booked the venues – who do you think is going to play Richard?'

'All right, who's playing Lady Anne?'

'Brian Glover.'

'The wrestler, Brian Glover?'

'If not him, Lisa Stansfield.'

'Has she ever acted before?'

'No, she'll be lovely and raw.'

'Have you asked her?'

'Not yet, but I can get to her – I know her neighbour.'

I left for my evening show, after this bracing and inspiring chat with my old chum. After a national tour I caught the production at the Riverside Studios in Hammersmith, as a guest of the then theatre critic Robert Butler, who had been asked to review it. Bobby and I had met on a production of *Exclusive* by Jeffrey Archer – he was working as script editor (not an easy task). Ishia Bennison played Lady Anne, Brian Glover played Buckingham and Barrie was a barnstorming Richard III. The whole thing played against a backdrop of builders' scaffolds and the show, as with many of Barrie's shows thereafter, opened with a wild clog dance. It was brilliant. He was brilliant. They were brilliant. And the entire audience was on its feet at the end.

Seeing that Bobby had also loved it I said, 'Let's go and meet Barrie.'

'I can't,' said Bobby, 'because I still have to write my notice.'

'He won't have a clue who you are.'

'OK.'

So we went to the bar, where we greeted Barrie, and I introduced Bobby.

'You're Robert Butler, *Independent on Sunday*.'

I was wrong – Barrie did know who Bobby was, and they ended up forming a mutually rewarding professional relationship, Bobby following Northern Broadsides to India and numerous other touring destinations to write about their performances.

For *Richard III* Barrie received a best production award and a best actor award, and he sold out at the Riverside. His company was launched. A few years later Northern Broadsides won the Millennium Award, worth £100,000, and both the Arts Council and the British Council recognised Barrie's work.

I witnessed his final production for Northern Broadsides, a farce, with a dance at the curtain call. It was at the Rose Theatre in Kingston, not a 'velvet venue' but a great modern theatre. I have great admiration for Barrie's work. Lots of people talk about doing such things – Barrie did it.

Peter Crouch & Glenda Jackson

In 1972 when I left RADA you could not get a job without an Equity card – and without a job – Catch 22. During my first year finals, playing Dust in *Next Time I'll Sing to You*, there was a knock on the dressing-room door. It was John Newman and Daphne Palmer of Newpalm Productions and they offered me a season at Chelmsford weekly rep – it carried an Equity card. I had been taken on by an agent, Peter Crouch Associates, so I asked Peter what I should do. 'Take it, darling. If you get a better offer I can always get you out of it.'

Each repertory company had two Equity cards to offer, one for an actor and one for an actress. Gold dust. You had to do forty-two weeks in the provinces on a provisional Equity card before you could appear in the West End or on television with a full Equity card. It was not a bad system – an apprenticeship.

In my final term I was asked to audition for Leeds Playhouse by David Carson, who had directed me in my finals. My audition was successful and I was offered a year's work, so I called Peter Crouch to ask him to negotiate my release from Chelmsford. 'Sorry darling, no luck – they're holding you to it. You'll have fun, and we'll come and see you.'

I went to RADA's principal, Hugh Cruttwell, and told him my tale of woe. 'That's nonsense, I'll call them.' He picked up the phone. 'Hello Mr Newman, you're not going to stand in the way of this young man's career, are you? Listen, I can get half a dozen much better actors to you this afternoon.' I was released – Roger Llewellyn got the Chelmsford gig, and loved it. Leeds became a two-year contract but there is still a part of me that would love to be able to say 'I did weekly rep.'

The Equity card was such a prize that some actors got theirs by working in strip clubs or on cruise ships. An Equity minimum wage still exists for an Equity contract but when the 'closed shop' became an 'open shop' the old crowd found it harder to make a living.

On the subject of wages, the BBC, who you could work for with a full Equity card, had a pay structure that included 'special highs' and 'special lows'. On one occasion I was cast as Platt in *The History of Mr Polly*. The actor cast as Polly had the possibility of a big film offer and was not prepared to commit until he knew. So the BBC in its wisdom had me on standby to take over as Polly if the film came through. In order to entice me I was offered 'a special high' for my Platt, £600 a week rather than £400. In the end Andrew Sachs didn't get his film so I was overpaid for Platt, a fee that haunted me for years to come as BBC TV directors would say 'I wanted you for this role in my series but I couldn't afford you as you're on a special high.'

Glenda Jackson, when she played Elizabeth in *Elizabeth R* was – or rather her agent Peter Crouch was – in negotiations with the BBC for her salary. Since she had last worked for the BBC, on a special low, she had won an Oscar, but as far as the BBC was concerned she was not a leading actor so could not be paid a leading actor's fee. There were heated discussions and threats of withdrawal and then the BBC came up with a suggestion.

'Does Miss Jackson need her house redecorated?'

'Why?'

'Because we, or rather the scenery department, could do that for her free of charge. Oh, and she will have a driver permanently at her disposal.'

The deal was signed but there was one further hitch in proceedings. When Glenda was asked to travel by train to one location, she found herself talking to the wardrobe mistress on the platform. As the train drew in, the wardrobe mistress said 'See you later' and got into a first-class carriage. Glenda had been issued with a second-class ticket.

On a later occasion our mutual agent Peter Crouch was asked by Trevor Nunn whether he had any influence with any Hollywood producers as he wanted to film his production of *Hedda Gabler*, starring Glenda Jackson, now a double Oscar-winner. Peter went to LA and made appointments with all the big shots – he got no takers. So he asked around: 'Who's the new kid on the block?' He was given a name and made an appointment. The conversation went something like this:

'We have a brilliant RSC production, starring the Oscar-winning Glenda Jackson, in a play by Henrik Ibsen.'

'Does it have a happy ending?'

'Well no, Hedda Gabler shoots herself at the end.'

'Would the author be interested in changing the ending?'

'Er no, he's dead.'

'Why did you come to me with this project?'

Deep breath from Peter.

'Because in Great Britain we hear that you are the most exciting producer in Hollywood.'

'Really…?'

They got the money and made the film.

When Glenda gave a eulogy at Peter Crouch's funeral she said that she had always determined that she would retire when Peter could no longer be her agent. Peter had represented her from day one and believed in her, and continued to reinforce his belief. 'When you crack it, they will want only you,' he told her. She told a story of coming home from LA after the premiere of *A Touch of Class*, most of which Peter had slept through. No sooner had the plane taken off than oxygen masks dropped down in front of every passenger. Peter turned to Glenda and just laughed. 'I was often asked why I stayed with Peter,' she said, 'and I would tell them that story to explain. He never took anything too seriously.'

I remember, early on in my career, asking Peter rather earnestly what he thought was the most important quality for an actor. He replied 'Attitude'.

Bill Fraser

RONALD EYRE INVITED me to play Dyson in his production of *When We Are Married*, opposite the great Bill Fraser. Ronald was the ultimate director's director. Michael Rudman once told me that he had come to England from America to get as far away from his parents and family as possible, to speak English and to study Ronald Eyre productions.

Over a drink before we started rehearsals I said to Bill, 'I am playing your sidekick, Dyson, and we are with the same agent. If I don't feed you a line properly, please let me know – don't beat about the bush.'

'I'm sure that won't be necessary.'

Bill had got only one lung and that was infected. At the time he was doing a television recording as Bert Baxter in *The Secret Diary of Adrian Mole* as well as rehearsing with us. He had arranged to rehearse for no more than an hour at a time and kept his driver waiting outside. His driver was an old friend, who I think had been in Variety. Bill had bought the car

Leslie Phillips, Reginald Beckwith and Bill Fraser on the set of *Doctor in Love*, 1960.

and had first call on his services; the rest of the time he used the car as a minicab.

At the first rehearsal we did of the opening scene of the second act, Bill asked, 'Ron, will they be smoking cigars after dinner?' 'I don't know yet,' said Ron. At the second rehearsal for that scene, Bill said, 'Do I remember rightly – they'll be smoking cigars, won't they?' to which Ron replied, 'Yes, I seem to remember something about that,' and asked the stage manager to make a note of it. At the third rehearsal of the scene Bill said, 'I'm just going to take one of these cigars, as they're here,' and disappeared under the canopy of his camera, puffing away at the cigar. In performance, as couples came in to be photographed he was taken by surprise and a cloud of smoke went up. That always got a big laugh from the audience.

I said to Bill, 'I see what you did there.' He replied, 'Comedy is a series of tricks carefully sewn together. Don't let anyone tell you anything different.'

Every night for six months we would sit in the wings for ten minutes before curtain up, and Bill would listen to the audience. I carried his equipment and he'd take it from me to make his entrance, to open the show. As he took the camera, with its wooden tripod and a bag, he'd say, 'Come on, Dr Footlights,' and on he'd sail, to give a top performance. It was a performance that won him an Olivier Award in 1986, an award picked up by his wife, Pamela Cundell, as by then Bill wasn't well enough to collect it himself.

He also got a round of applause for a bit of business that he added during the run. One member of the cast had a purple feather boa so when Bill opened the second act he'd pick up a purple feather that he'd planted during the interval and say, 'Hello, has there been a purple duck in here?'

One night, with a full house as usual, Paul and Linda McCartney were in. The following day I got a call from my agent who said, ‘Paul McCartney wants to screen-test you to play his father in *Give My Regards to Broad Street*.’ Bill said, ‘Go in your costume.’ ‘But I’ve got a stick-on moustache!’ ‘Wear that too – what he’s seen is what he wants.’

Bill went on to say that when he had gone to audition for Bert Baxter he had got his driver to stop outside the gates to Thames Television. He asked him to look after this false teeth and changed into an old coat before going in – ‘Give them what they want.’ I didn’t heed his advice and I didn’t get the part. He did get the part of Bert Baxter so I should have listened, and been brave enough.

When Bill was nominated for his Olivier Award he asked me to lunch with him at Simpson’s in the Strand at 12 noon on a Thursday, before our matinée. When I arrived, he was there to meet me, resplendent in a blazer.

‘What will you have? I’m having a gin and tonic.’

‘Oh.’

I had planned to stick to soft drinks but could see that was not an option.

‘The same please.’

‘A large gin and tonic for Mr Bourke.’

We moved through to the glorious dining-room and were seated comfortably.

‘I like Chablis with my oysters. Do you?’

‘That sounds lovely.’

When the roast beef came round on a silver trolley,

Bill ordered 'A bottle of Châteauneuf-du-Pape to go with that, I think.'

And to me, 'Always remember that there is no such thing as a free lunch – except for this one – and one day, you'll do the same for someone else.'

He talked about the sum of money he would be leaving to his wife Pam – 'She will always be comfortably off' – and indeed she was. Bill had always been in work and had run a business, a sweet shop and tobacconist for example, on the side. He was never unemployed and ever careful. For some years he ran the Connaught Theatre in Worthing as a weekly repertory theatre, and when he put on *Hamlet* he would pay the lead actor a week's salary to learn it.

At the end of our lunch Bill ordered brandies with our coffees – much needed coffee. I was swaying as we stood outside on the pavement and Bill hailed a taxi to the theatre. When we got there I had another coffee and a cold shower, telling myself as I looked at my reflection in the make-up mirror and stuck on my moustache: 'You can do this!' I was extremely tiddly.

Bill and I met as usual in the wings; Bill showing no signs of wear and tear. I handed him his photographic equipment and on he went, brilliant as ever. I felt sure that the audience would be able to tell that I was drunk and, as I was playing a journalist, tried to convince myself that this was in character. That was the only time I have ever had a drink before performing but I wouldn't have missed that lunch for a wilderness of monkeys. I learnt some invaluable lessons from Bill, in particular the need to have a second string to your bow, an alternative source of income.

My role was over just after the interval, which caused one critic to write, 'Peter Bourke is excellent as Dysart – what a pity he has such an early bath.' But that early bath meant that I had a chance to play bridge against Timothy West and Prunella Scales. My partner was Julian Wadham and we played beneath the stage, so that Tim and the others could hear their cues. Tim would say 'Three no trump', go on stage and play a scene, come back and Pru would bid back to him. Our games were accompanied in the later months of the run by drinks, each of us taking it in turn to buy wine. One night Tim introduced us to Special Brew – never again will I drink Special Brew. The curtain call was a challenge. Bowing was fine but standing upright was a real struggle. I took the bus home that night – usually I would run, as I was training for the London Marathon.

Britt: 12,755 and Counting

In 1983 my best chum Nicky Henson invited me to supper: 'It's me and three girls.'

We ate in the garden of his girlfriend Marguerite Porter's house. Britt was wearing a T-shirt and red shorts. It was love at first sight! Nicky and Marguerite brought us together twice more before Britt went to work at a polio and leprosy hospital in Old Delhi to 'put something back'.

While she was away I went to watch Marguerite dance Juliet in Kenneth MacMillan's *Romeo and Juliet* at the Hippodrome in Bristol, and invited her to stay with my parents in Shepton Mallet after the show. I asked her about Britt, when she was due back and, most importantly, what her telephone number was. The day Britt returned I phoned and asked her out. She said she was packing to go home to Norway for the summer.

Britt (© Antony Dufort).

'Well, if you get finished in time, call me and we can meet.'

I got the call and we met, Britt in her smart Alfa

Romeo, me in my battered Beetle. Over Peking duck we knew we would be together for ever.

Britt was the physiotherapist for the touring company, Sadler's Wells Royal Ballet. I joined her in Bombay and we travelled to Jaipur and Udaipur for two weeks' holiday, ending up at the Lake Palace Hotel, a beautiful white building that looks as if it floats on the lake. We were met on shore and rowed out to the landing stage.

'Mr Bourke I am so sorry, your room is being redecorated. We are so sorry, sir. But we have found you another room.'

We were led across marble walkways until we arrived at a pair of huge double doors, oak with ornate brass fittings, through those and into a room with a vast bed on ropes, stained glass windows on three sides, flowers everywhere, low couches round the walls and the lake water lapping outside. The whole exquisite place had been designed by and for the architect of the Taj Mahal. This was the bridal suite.

'This is wonderful, thank you. But how much is it?'

'Our mistake, sir, so the same price as your original room.'

We were flabbergasted. We had three glorious days: outings to town, trips on the lake in their magnificent boat, a visit to Elephant Island, a pool just for us to swim in. It became our honeymoon, one that could never be beaten. On the fourth day we left to take the long train journey back to Bombay. We had ordered a car to take us to the station and after an hour, when it still hadn't arrived, we realised that we were in danger of missing the train.

We turned to each other and I said, 'We'll never come here again. Shall we ask if we can stay two more days?'

The boat picked us up and took us back across the lake. We were met by the manager. 'Mr Bourke, how lovely to see you again, sir. Your usual room?'

We had two more wonderful days in that fairy-tale place, and paid nothing more than we would have paid for our original booking. The last time I checked, that suite cost £4,500 a night.

All the same, wherever you've been, in my experience it is lovely to get home.

In 1988 Britt began to retrain, over five years, as a performance psychologist. She has now worked with Olympic athletes, ballet dancers, footballers, snooker players, injury-plagued runners – the list is endless. It includes the English rugby team the year they won in Australia, the British coxless four who won Olympic gold, Olaf Tufte, Norwegian double gold medallist for single sculling, and the handball girls who also won Olympic gold for Norway. In fact, her Norwegian Winter Olympic team won thirty-seven medals, not bad for a country of 5 million. I have never placed a bet on any of Britt's athletes but I wish I had. Recently she worked with two of the key players for the Chelsea women's football team and said, 'That went well.' Chelsea broke Arsenal's eight-year dominance a couple of days later.

Britt had applied to Goldsmiths, where she believes they took her because she was Norwegian and they thought she would pay foreign student's fees. When they asked her what she would read with psychology she said, 'anthropology'.

'What branch of anthropology?'

'Social anthropology.'

'Interesting,' they said, and offered her a place.

She'd said this because while she was sitting and waiting she'd seen a notice advertising a social anthropology field trip. Britt is now a Fellow of Goldsmiths.

Here's Sir Clive Woodward on Britt:

> Simon pulled out his prescription pad and began scribbling on the front.
>
> 'This is the phone number of a friend of mine you should go and see. Her name is Britt Tajet-Foxell. She is the top performance psychologist at the Royal Ballet. I think she can help. Give me twenty-four hours to speak to her first and then give her a call.'
>
> With a name like that I had to go and see her. I wondered what a psychologist would do at the Royal Ballet. It sounded really interesting. As

I later found out, Britt also works in the High Performance Centre of the Norwegian Olympic team and is responsible for some hundred elite athletes going to Athens this year. Thankfully, Britt was in town and offered to see me on Thursday, the team's day off before the Test match.

As I explained my situation Britt listened, nodded carefully in places, and asked insightful questions. Just talking with her helped me feel so much better, but she also suggested eight steps I could take to correct the situation. Britt and I only chatted for an hour, but in that time my whole perception of England rugby changed. She helped me to see all the good things we'd been doing in the elite set-up, and she urged me to ignore completely the harsh criticism in the press. She had a good point: my detractors would always be there, no matter what I did. I appreciated Britt's care and concern, but what really won me over was when she suggested I should play more golf, at least twice a week like I used to – my game had fallen away as my coaching intensity had risen over the past few years.

Since that meeting, we've kept in regular contact and Britt has become a good source for insight into the team. I followed her recommendations from our first chat and within a few weeks my sleep was right back to normal. Then again, perhaps it helped playing three pivotal matches – and winning.

Jeffrey Archer & Paul Scofield

I WAS OUT of work when the phone rang one day.

'Hello Peter, it's Michael – Michael Rudman.'

'Hello Michael, how lovely to hear from you.'

'I'm directing a play, a new play, about newspapers.'

'Sounds exciting.'

'I've already got Paul Scofield and Eileen Atkins, so I thought I should give you a call.'

'Gosh!'

'Yes. I want you to play the sports editor. I'll bike you over a script.'

'With that cast and with you directing, I could save you time and say yes now.'

'Read it first.'

'Who wrote it?'

'Jeffrey Archer,' said Michael, and put the phone down.

I knew Michael had turned down Jeffrey's first play,

Paul Scofield in 1974.

Beyond Reasonable Doubt, but not before suggesting that the acts should be played in reverse order. The script arrived within half an hour. I read it and said yes. It had a large cast and a rather clever 'whodunnit' plot – I could see why Michael had agreed to do it.

Michael asked me to do some research at Mirror Group Newspapers by undertaking work experience on the sports desk. 'We're having a read-through two months before we start rehearsals. Please bring experiences, phrases, ideas, so that Jeffrey can do rewrites – with authentic details.'

I duly arranged to go into the *Mirror*, coincidentally on a day when England were playing Albania at football. I arrived at the paper's offices, just off Fleet Street, on the dot of 10. The sports editor greeted me with, 'You look like a Sancerre man to me. Two bottles of Sancerre for Mr Bourke – now, let's get you started. What is Albania famous for?'

'I'm afraid I don't know.'

'King Zog!'

'Oh.'

'So now give us a headline.'

'Is this Zogger?' I offered.

'You're in the wrong fucking game, son,' he said, and proceeded to rewrite the headline in black felt tip, the pen held in his fist.

The phone rang. It was someone trying to sell him some scandalous gossip. He listened and said 'No', then turned to me and said, 'You need a bottle of Dettol to wash the phone after speaking to that guy.'

Robert Maxwell hovered for a while and, when he was out of earshot, the sports editor said, 'He wants to be on the back pages as well as the front.'

I sipped my Sancerre while he told me about his three great loves: 'My children, Arsenal and my wife, in no particular order,' before suggesting that we go out to lunch.

'Don't we need to listen to the game,' I asked.

'No, I pay people to do that.'

Lunch, or rather liquid lunch, was champagne at a wine bar, my host buying two bottles of Moët at a time. He asked the *Fred Basset* cartoonist to join us.

'I'm banned from here.'

'We'll shield you, and you're our guest.'

Six of us drank eight bottles of champagne. I could barely stand as I bought the last round. Crossing the road on the way back to the office, my new friend said 'You have to be sharp for twenty minutes a day in this job.' The following day when I read the article, the headline was: Thank Zog for that.

I staggered back to Brixton and started, with difficulty, to climb Brixton Hill, where I met a neighbour coming towards me. He was a *Guardian* photographer at the time, so no explanation was needed of my condition after a day's work experience at the *Mirror*.

'I'll just see you home – I don't think Britt would ever forgive me if I don't.'

On the day of our first rehearsal, new scripts arrived by bike at 8 in the morning. They bore no resemblance to the script we'd read two months before. Our rehearsal room was in Pettit House on the Embankment at Chelsea. Our read-through began after a short talk from Michael Rudman and as soon as we'd finished, John Stride walked out, saying 'This is not what I signed up for.'

At the lunchbreak, everyone but me and Paul Scofield went to the pub. I had brought my packed lunch and so had Paul. During these rehearsal breaks I was careful to respect his privacy, but I discovered, like me, that he made his own bread and, a little later, and also like me, that he cut his own hair. Although, for the part of the newspaper editor, he had gone and had it cut at Trumpers – that's where he felt his character would go.

After lunch, Michael announced that Alec McCowen had accepted John Stride's role. I was thrilled as I had worked with Alec at the National Theatre on *The Browning Version* and *Harlequinade*, and had seen him play the Fool to Scofield's King Lear directed by Peter Brook.

The play opened in Bath and was a sell-out – Paul's name endorsing Jeffrey Archer's. The reviews didn't matter. We toured to Manchester and then came to London, where we played at the Strand Theatre (now the Novello), to an exceptionally glamorous first-night audience, most of whom joined us at the party afterwards in a hotel on Leicester Square. The guests included most of Margaret Thatcher's Cabinet, and Joan Collins, who I hadn't seen since I filmed *The Stud* with her and she had very kindly got the script-writers to write an extra scene for me.

The reviews were terrible. At the party I had found myself in a conversation with Paul Scofield and Eileen Atkins.

'Paul, what do you say when people ask you why you did this?'

'I say that I am always being asked to play Lear and the classics but not often asked to do new plays.'

One thinks of all the wonderful new plays that Paul did do – *A Man for All Seasons*, *Amadeus*, and a marvellous two-hander, *Savages*, at the Criterion in the early 70s with Ben Kingsley.

But Paul the great actor was also an outrageously naughty 'corpser', in fact brilliant at making other people corpse. He could make his face do terrible things when turned upstage, while his downstage face was serious and prophet-like. When he had successfully made you laugh helplessly, with a beautifully innocent expression he would say, 'I could see you were in a bit of difficulty out there. I do hope it was nothing I have done.'

At the Strand we started the show early so that Paul could get the last train back to his cottage in Balcombe. A cab would pick him up at the stage door and take him to the station. On one of these evenings, Paul told us that he was travelling home, smoking his pipe and reading his paper. A man got into his carriage and said, 'Don't tell me, don't tell me. Just a minute. It's Paul Scofield, isn't it?'

'Yes,' puff, puff, and back to his paper.

'Paul, can I call you Paul? You may not remember but we've worked together.'

'Oh, remind me.'

'It was in *A Man for All Seasons*. When you got off the barge at Hampton Court, there were two men sitting on the quayside. One of them was me!'

'Oh,' puff, puff, and back to the paper.

'I've got a question for you, Paul.'

'Oh?'

'Yes. My question is: why do we do it, eh?'

Eileen Atkins, on hearing this, said, 'Can I tell you my Alec Guinness story?'

'Please,' said Paul.

'Alec Guinness got into a cab and the driver said, "Don't tell me, I'll get it, you're David Nixon the conjuror, aren't you?"

'"No," said Alec, "I'm not." Looking at him in his rear view mirror, the driver said, "Bet you wish you were!"'

We needed to boost bookings after our very poor reviews – one of which said that restaurants in the vicinity of the Strand Theatre were embarrassed to find theatre-goers turning up for dinner at the interval rather than after the performance. So the management asked Paul's wife if he would appear on *This is Your Life*. She flatly refused on his behalf, so it was agreed that it would be Alec McCowen who would be ambushed by the appearance of Michael Aspel, holding his red book.

We were all bussed to the studio in Teddington as surprise guests. The show consisted mainly of Alec's aunts saying nice things about him, and turned out to be extremely safe and bland. So much so that Alec agreed to its being shown only if he was able to say at the beginning that he was a gay man whose lover, Geoffrey Burridge, had died of AIDS. The show was pulled, and the play closed soon afterwards.

To soften the blow, Jeffrey Archer invited us to a last-night party at his penthouse flat in Vauxhall. We had champagne and cottage pie and admired the art collection. When I left, he walked me to the lift and said, 'That suit you're wearing is too good for a jobbing actor.' I didn't trouble myself to explain that I had worn it in a series of *Gentlemen and Players* and bought it afterwards for the princely sum of £50.

John Gielgud

PATIENCE COLLIER, WONDERFUL actress and *grande dame* of the theatre, married to a professional businessman, living in Campden Hill Road, Notting Hill, had an eye for the young men. 'Come round after rehearsals and we can go through your lines.'

In 1974 she was playing Betsey Trotwood in a BBC television series of *David Copperfield*, in which I was playing Traddles. Arriving late for rehearsal one day, she apologised and said, 'I'm sorry I'm late but I had an interview for a job, arranged by John Gielgud.' She started to giggle.

'What's so funny?' we asked.

'Well, after the interview I called Sir John from the nearest phone box to thank him for recommending me and to tell him that it had gone well. He said, "Oh good, I'm so pleased – but pray that Athene [Seyler] gets it. She needs the work!"'

Timothy Bateson, who was playing Mr Dick, said,

'Can I tell my Johnny G story?'

'Yes please,' was the general answer.

'Well, I was at Victoria Station one day and spotted him coming towards me.

'"Hello Sir John, how are you?"

'"Oh, terrible, terrible! It's the travelling you see. What I really need is a little pied-à-terre in London. It wouldn't really matter how poky and squalid it was – is there anything going in your block?"'

Gielgud was infamous for gaffes. For example, he went to see Richard Burton as Hamlet and didn't like the performance. When he went round to Burton's dressing-room afterwards, Gielgud was confronted by the star in just his underpants. A little flustered, he said, 'Oh, I'll come back when you're better, I mean dressed.' But the meeting inspired him to suggest that he might direct Burton as Hamlet. Laurence Olivier, hearing about this, asked Peter O'Toole to play Hamlet in *his* production. Two healthy rival actors, directed by two healthy rival actors – for a shoot-out. Both great productions and great performances by all accounts.

That story was told to me by the distinguished actor Anthony Nicholls, my then father-in-law. He went on to tell me another story, about a party that Gielgud gave to introduce him and other friends to his new boyfriend, Rupert. As Anthony was leaving the party he said to Gielgud:

'I so enjoyed meeting Rupert.'

John Gielgud and Margaret Leighton in
Much Ado About Nothing, 1950s.

'Rupert, who's Rupert?'

'Your new boyfriend.'

'Oh! Oh! Oh! His name isn't Rupert.'

'But that was how you introduced him to me.'

'Did I? Oh dear, that's the name we give his cock.'

When he was working for the great director Peter Brook, playing Oedipus in *Oedipus Rex*, Peter asked the cast members to come to the front of the stage and say the worst thing that they could imagine happening, as a rehearsal exercise. Sir John hung back. Finally, every other actor had spilled his guts.

'John, it's your turn now.'

'Oh, if I must, I must. You want me to say the worst thing I can possibly imagine happening? Here it is: we open in two weeks.'

I am now the Honorary Treasurer of the Actors' Benevolent Fund. Many years ago Sir John was our President. It was at the time of his arrest in a gents' loo in Piccadilly tube station. He was erased from the Council, but when he died he left a large sum of money to the Fund, and his sketchbook, which has been well mined for greetings cards. That's forgiveness and greatness.

Margaret Thatcher

SIR MICHAEL HAVERS, father of Nigel, was bombed out of his Wimbledon flat by the IRA when he was MP for Wimbledon and Attorney General in Margaret Thatcher's government. Fortunately he was at his house in Norfolk that weekend. Lord Carrington offered Sir Michael his flat, behind the RAC Club and overlooking the Mall.

It was Michael's turn to have the Cabinet to dinner and to spice things up a little he asked Nigel to invite some of his actor friends. Michael had established that Thatcher's favourite actor was Peter Bowles, and he was duly summoned. I was also included and when I came out of the lift, Michael said, 'Stay here, Maggie's just on her way up.' We waited, the lift came back up and out of the doors stepped Margaret Thatcher and Peter Bowles.

'Prime Minister' said Michael, 'this is Peter Bowles. Peter, this is our Prime Minister, Margaret Thatcher.'

'We have been intimate already,' replied Peter.

'No we have not,' snapped Thatcher and swept off.

Unfortunately they were seated next to each other at dinner, during which Thatcher kept her back resolutely turned on Peter.

My other recollection of Margaret Thatcher concerns my good friend, sculptor Antony Dufort. He won the competition to make a bronze replacement for a marble sculpture by Neil Simmons – decapitated in an act of politically motivated vandalism.

Lady Thatcher modelled for Antony several times, in the River Room of the House of Lords, posing as if mid-speech. When Antony thanked her for being so helpful, she said: 'Well, it's in my own best interest…'

Antony was at the same time working on a tribute sculpture to the Nottinghamshire coal miners and collieries. That work showed a young miner on one knee, squinting at the height of the flame in his Davey lamp. Thatcher admired his strong arms in a photograph of the in-progress sculpture. When talking to his miner clients, Antony decided it best to keep quiet about what he was doing at Westminster.

To get the correct speaking shape for Thatcher's lips, Antony asked her to say a word beginning with a 'B'. Without hesitation she responded: 'Britain … Britain … *Great* Britain.'

The magnificent bronze, with jabbing forefinger, echoing her famous final speech as Prime Minister in the House of Commons, stands in Members' Lobby

The Thatcher bronze (© Antony Dufort).

of the Palace of Westminster. As she unveiled the sculpture with aid of the Speaker, she said: 'I might have preferred iron, but bronze will do … And it won't rust.' Cue roars of laughter from the assembled crowd of politicians of all stripes.

A different and, at 12 feet, much larger sculpture

of Thatcher by Dufort stands opposite a huge head of Churchill, by Oscar Nemon, in the Los Angeles sculpture garden of property tycoon Harlan Crow.

Among the surrounding trees lurk huge, orphaned sculptures of dead Communist leaders and deposed dictators.

Endgame

When I was at RADA we used to get free tickets to shows that weren't selling well, when they were 'papering the house'. The most memorable was a production of *Endgame* at the Shaw Theatre.

The cast included Trevor Peacock, who I later worked with at Stratford, Patricia Hayes, who I later worked with in *When We Are Married*, and Harold Innocent, who I later worked with both on television and in *On the Razzle* at the National Theatre. I loved the play, the production and the performances, without quite knowing why. So much did I enjoy it that I went again the following night.

Years later, when Britt qualified as a performance psychologist after three years at Goldsmiths and two years doing her masters in occupational psychology, she asked me what I had always wanted to do. I said, 'I'd like to be actor-manager on a tour of *Endgame* and play Clov.'

The first call was to Samuel Beckett's agents, Curtis

As Clov, with Brian Matthew as Nagg and John Quentin as Hamm; *Endgame*, Arts Theatre, London 1994.

Brown, to persuade them to sell me the rights. We had a meeting, and I was asked to sign a contract agreeing to follow Beckett's stage instructions to the letter, a requirement stipulated for all his plays. I paid £750 as an advance against 10 per cent of the box office.

I had recently worked at the Salisbury Playhouse in Alan Bennett's *Single Spies*, in which my co-star was an actor called John Quentin. He had read English at Oxford and is a fine poet. His stature, voice, everything was right for the role of Hamm – also, I hope he won't mind me saying, his sexual ambiguity. He agreed to join me on the adventure. It was he who suggested the sculptor Miles Bodimeade to design the set or, as he put it, 'the sculptural shapes' – the windows, the wheelchair (which became a throne) and the all-important dustbins to house Nagg and Nell, Hamm's elderly parents. The wheelchair/throne depicted the New York skyline and could be moved about. It was all falling into place. I was keen to have an acting couple to play Nagg and Nell. I thought of Michael Denison and Dulcie Gray, and then I thought of Brian Matthew and his wife Pamela Wickington – I had worked with them in a production of *The Merry Wives of Windsor* at Chichester.

Brian had trained at RADA but got into radio during the War and became a hugely successful DJ, partly responsible for the early success of the Beatles, and had been in partnership with Brian Epstein, the Beatles's manager. Apart from being a good actor, Brian was a big catch – ideal for local radio on our planned tour. Pamela was excellent casting too, and they had each other.

We started with a read-through in Brian and Pamela's private theatre in their house in Orpington and then rehearsed at the Battersea Arts Centre, where our tour was to end. The opening night was in Salisbury, a sell-out despite the publicity department failing to display Clive Francis's beautifully designed posters. In fact we were so sold out that there wasn't a ticket for the local *Guardian* theatre critic.

'That's all right, we don't need him.'

'But he hasn't reviewed here for years.'

I remembered that he had a reputation for not liking anything. As it happened they did find him a ticket, and he did praise the show, so it was lovely to be touring with a good review from the *Guardian*.

Our tour finished at the Sheffield Crucible, where my old friend Michael Rudman was artistic director, and along the way we did one-night stands at Canterbury, Chipping Norton and various other places. All very satisfying for the 'angels' who had invested in the show, and helpful for me, as I was performing, managing and producing, with Britt as my sleeping partner.

The reviews at Sheffield were so good that Michael took me to lunch to ask what I wanted to do next. One of the reviews said, 'Why does it take the whimsically named Fair Play Theatre Company to bring us the best thing we have had here in years?'

I travelled in a van I had borrowed from my neighbour, which had failed its MOT. I had said to him, 'If I can make it roadworthy, can I borrow it for the tour?' and he had agreed.

Fortunately I had the most brilliant mechanic friend called Charlie.

'Charlie, I've been lent this van for nothing for the tour of *Endgame*.'

'I can see why.'

'It failed its MOT.'

'As I say, I can see why.'

Charlie was a drama-loving garage man who had

worked on tanks during the War. His favourite playwright was Tom Stoppard and I'd gained a certain amount of credibility with him when he came to the National Theatre to see me in Stoppard's *On the Razzle*. That evening we ended up in an Italian restaurant in Stockwell where Charlie was well known and paid the bill from a fat roll of notes. I think the real highlight for him was meeting Bob Hoskins in the Green Room.

For £75 Charlie fixed my neighbour's huge VW van to transport the wheelchair/throne, the two dustbins and the tall steel windows, one prison-like and one ecclesiastical. I bonded with the van on our way to Salisbury, where we had our technical run-through and where I bought a simple but brilliant lighting design from the resident lighting designer. Simon Limbrick, another Brixton neighbour, wrote and recorded a beautifully composed soundtrack. In each town we went to Brian did a spot on the local radio station and talked about the Beatles and our show in the same breath to adoring audiences. There were no serious mishaps although in Sheerness we couldn't use the throne as it wouldn't go through the door so had to borrow a wheelchair from a local old people's home. I felt sure that Beckett would approve. And we were selling out every night.

I drove back down the motorway from Sheffield with a great sense of relief – we had made a profit, played seven theatres, the van hadn't broken down, the actors got on with each other. And so we opened to the national press at the Battersea Arts Centre, and got astonishingly good reviews. We had four columns in the *Financial Times* saying that it was Samuel Beckett's best play and why had it taken so long to be presented as a stand-alone evening. It praised the production and the cast and I wept when I read it – certainly none of us was doing it for the money.

We were attracting a really exciting audience. One night, Steve Coppell, the legendary football player and manager, was in the box office queue along with Alec Guinness. Coppell was asked by the theatre critic Robert Butler what he thought of the play, and answered, 'It seems like it was written by someone halfway between drunk and sober.'

We were offered a transfer by two West End theatres and chose the smaller Arts Theatre for a limited season, one reason being that it was where *Waiting for Godot* was first performed. A further stroke of luck was that *Endgame* was on both the A level and the Open University syllabus and we were the only production in town.

I had no budget for publicity so had to be creative, sticking our posters to lampposts and on the side of derelict buildings late at night, and I paid a friend, Alfie Howard, to walk around Leicester Square wearing a sandwich board with the poster stuck on both sides. Alfie was the Town Cryer of

Lambeth and had been a music hall star since the age of six, working for the comedian and impresario Fred Karno and making a lifelong friend of the then tap dancer, later silent movie star, Charlie Chaplin. His act, aged six, was at the Empress Theatre and involved him coming on stage with a pint pot, going up to a barman behind a counter, handing him the pot to be filled and walking off with it. Moments later he came back:

'My Dad says this is full of element.'

'Don't you mean sediment, son?'

'I don't know what the hell he meant, but that's what he said he meant.'

At the time Alfie was his family's breadwinner as his father was an alcoholic. When theatre work dried up for him he was caught stealing a loaf of bread and a tin of spam and sent to Borstal, which he described as his university education. Alfie 'cried' *Endgame* all round Leicester Square, ringing his bell in his official capacity as the Lambeth Town Cryer: 'Oyez, oyez!' Beckett loved music hall and wrote *Endgame* in music hall rhythms – I always wondered whether he might have seen Alfie at the Empress in Brixton.

Our other advertising was a competition in the *Independent* newspaper – the first twenty people to book day seats got them for £10. On slack days we just let it run. Being the actor-manager the sales were my top priority. I had arrived at the Arts Theatre on my first day and the box office lady was on the phone. 'Never mind,' I thought, 'I can wait.' And wait I did. Eventually I thought 'She's not selling tickets,' and I went up to the window.

'Excuse me, I'm the manager of *Endgame* and I've taken a huge personal financial risk on the show. I can't have the phone line busy while you're talking to a friend.'

'Sorry.'

'I'll make you an offer – I'll put you and your staff on 2 per cent of any tickets you sell.'

She agreed, saying, 'That's never happened before,' and stayed off the phone.

The run built up gently. As I stood on stage as Clov in the opening tableau, out of the corner of my eye I could count the full rows of seats in the stalls – 10 was break-even, 11 was champagne time.

Britt and I were in this together and often discussed which of our Roy Petley paintings we would have to sell and in which order. Britt had bought these paintings off the railings in Piccadilly for a few hundred pounds, rather than the tens of thousands they are worth today. We didn't have to sell any, thanks to a brilliant review from Nick Curtis in the then powerful *Time Out*, as a result of which we sold £1,000 worth of tickets in one hour – giving the box office their cut of course.

Endgame finished its run at the Arts Theatre in July 1994, with our painting collection intact. On our way to the Harwich ferry for a much needed holiday,

Britt took a picture of me and our daughter Poppy under the brilliant photograph by Nobby Clark of me and John Quentin on stage, still surrounded by lights.

Fair Play Theatre Company

After the West End premiere of *Endgame* friends asked me what my newly formed company would be doing next.

While my daughter Poppy was at Sudbourne Primary School the head teacher, Susan Scarsbrook – a wonderful head, I think, because she expected more from every child, parent and member of staff than they were planning to give – asked me to put on a performance to celebrate the Victorians. 'I'll do an old-time music hall show,' I said. 'Brixton was the centre of music hall and Variety – Fred Karno owned the Clockwork Studios, known as the Fun Factory, where he trained clowns, and performers including Charlie Chaplin. That's what I'll do.'

Well, I didn't think much more about it until September of that year when Susan (I had permission to call her Susan as I was one of her trusted governors) said, 'I've set the date for the music hall show.' It was two weeks away.

I knew that the comic actor Len Howe and his wife Audrey Maye lived close to the school. Audrey's mother Elsie May Warden and Freddie Frinton had done the great New Year entertainment *Dinner for One* and had passed the rights to Len and Audrey, who were paid £5,000 to resurrect it for a private performance for a Swedish bank, long after they had retired. They agreed to perform, and Audrey to direct. I started calling local mates – Robert Bathurst signed up, as did Mary Chiltern, Sean Seymour and, most importantly, Alfie Howard, who was to compère and do his parrot gag, that he had got from Fred Karno. It was later adapted and taken up by Freddie 'Parrot Face' Davies.

In the school staff room at rehearsals we discussed the running order. Audrey said 'No-one will want to follow Len.' 'I don't mind,' said Robert Bathurst. 'No really,' said Audrey, 'He's an old-timer.' The act he was going to do was his drunk act, which involved him swallowing a lighted cigarette and, after a lot of brilliant business, bringing it back, still alight.

We each did our acts – mine as the great McAllister, a failed actor who sent himself up on the halls, to much acclaim – an act I stole from my days as a student assistant stage manager at Lincoln Theatre Royal.

We rehearsed our routines and songs, with a bit

of movement and then – we were on, for one night only! It was a packed house, everyone sitting on children's school chairs, at small tables, all clapping and joining in whenever they got the chance. By half-time we were having a ball, and assembled in the staff room. But where was our star? Len wasn't there. We sent someone to run and knock on his door. He'd been fast asleep but woke up, unfazed and clutching a half-bottle of whisky.

Robert went on to do a bit of stand-up, wearing a false moustache and a blue checked suit. Coming off to loud applause he passed Len, who said 'Well done son, but try doing that twice nightly,' then went on and fell into his act. It was fifteen minutes of pure clowning – running his hat across his chest and catching it, trying to strike matches that refused to light, finally striking one, putting it back in the box, lighting a cigarette that spooked him, making him gasp and swallow it, putting the matches back in his pocket, missing the pocket, coughing, producing the cigarette still smoking – another fifteen minutes of wild applause, a final full company song and that was that.

Robert (Bobby) Butler was in the audience, at that time the theatre critic for the *Independent on Sunday*, and he wrote about Len's performance in his annual round-up – 'The best twelve minutes of theatre I saw this year was Len Howe's drunk act at Sudbourne Primary School's Old Time Music Hall.'

I said to Bobby, 'What do you want to write for the Fair Play Theatre Company?' and he said, 'Something like that, something where people sit around at tables, having a drink and being entertained.' 'Could it be a Dickens show?' I asked him. 'With a small cast, everyone playing lots of parts. A minimal set – tables and chairs becoming a horse and cart, a prison cell, a pawn shop?'

He came up with five playlets from Dickens's *Sketches by Boz* and we performed in the bar at the Battersea Arts Centre, ending up being compared very favourably in the press with the RSC's *Christmas Carol* that was playing at the Barbican.

I then commissioned Bobby to write a play for us to take to the Edinburgh Festival, at the urging of his mother, Lord Justice Elizabeth Butler-Sloss – 'Can't you get Bobby to write another play for you? Otherwise he's just doing journalism.' He came up with a wonderful piece – original, creative and brilliant – *Our State Tomorrow*, a quote from *Romeo and Juliet*. In an imagined after-story, Friar Laurence and Lady Capulet meet in a basement café as they take cover from fighting in 1945, as the Allies are relieving Verona. Thrown together, they start to apportion blame for what happened earlier, witnessed by an American GI and a female war correspondent who has heard of the love story and its tragic end, and can't believe that she has two of the principal characters to interview as bombs fall. It was pick of the week, a week in which we drew audiences every night. You don't make money in Edinburgh but you do gain courage.

The Fair Play Theatre Company went on to produce *Bring on the Dancing Poodles* by Douglas McFadden, directed by Ian McElhinney. We were all hoping it would become the next *Stones in His Pockets*, Ian's previous big hit. It was good – it still could. A successful actor and an amateur actor who admires him have a chance meeting at a bus stop in Norfolk. The amateur actor has played all his hero's parts. Douglas and I toured it and brought it into the Players' Theatre in London.

For a couple of hundred pounds you can start a company limited by guarantee and once you have one, as an actor you need never feel out of work again.

Algernon Bourke

My ancestor Algernon Bourke was the Recorder of Cork and the Earl of Mayo. He bought St Mary's Bramber, near Shoreham in Sussex, and where a wing of the house had burnt down he built a music room for his wife Gwendolen to give piano recitals.

A frequent weekend guest was their old friend from Dublin days, Oscar Wilde, who went on to immortalise Algernon and Gwendolen in *The Importance of Being Earnest*. Many of the other characters in his brilliant comedy are named after railway stations on his journey to Bramber, on the Worthing line, which took you in those days through Bracknell (although I believe the Brighton line may have been more direct). There are wonderful Spy cartoons of the three of them together, hanging in the hall at St Mary's.

I discovered all these facts when I was invited to take my production of *Sketches by Boz*, based on the first works of fiction by Charles Dickens, written for magazine publication when he was a very young man, and perform in the music room. My older daughter Emily and her husband Jimmy got married from St Mary's, with their three children in attendance.

My connections with Ireland started with my grandfather, John Bertram Bourke, who built up a family business in Kanturk, Co. Cork, eventually buying his final business in the town, a bar, which was to become his downfall. Bourke's grocers is still there today, but the ironmongers and the mill are long gone. John Bourke, the oldest son, and heir to the family seat, Assolas, was unceremoniously bought a £10 ticket to Australia when time spent in the newly acquired bar got the better of him. On the boat to Australia he met my grandmother and my great-aunt, the daughters of great-grandfather Williams, of Williams Irish linen business in Bristol. He had three girls and they were among the first women to have a university education. So passionate about education was Aunt Molly that she was dragging her sister, Ethel Rose, to Australia to found the Fröbel early years learning department at Melbourne University. On the long sea voyage, Ethel and John became romantically attached and John proposed marriage. Her acceptance was on condition that he sober up and get an education. John duly sobered up and, with financial help from Ethel's father, qualified as a doctor – over a lengthy engagement period.

They married and, on returning to England, John put up his brass plaque in Bristol, building a sizeable practice. They had a cook, a housekeeper, a gardener but regrettably not a chauffeur, as John had bought one of Bristol's first motor cars. He was discovered drunk, driving round and round the city centre tramway, the wheels of the car having locked in the tram tracks. It made the newspapers and Dr John Bourke had to leave town with his family. They moved to Crewkerne near Yeovil and once again he put up his brass plaque and built a successful practice. One afternoon, after a boozy lunch, John got on a train, passed out and ended up in Glasgow. My grandmother threw him out.

My Aunt Molly, or rather my father's Aunt Molly, felt responsible for my grandparents' meeting. She said, 'If I hadn't asked my sister to come and help me in Australia this would never have happened.' She bought number 14, The Paragon in Clifton in Bristol for £500 and gave the top two floors to my father (aged eight at the time) and his mother. She lived on the two floors below and they had a couple living in the basement who cooked and cleaned and did odd jobs.

My father was sent to Christ's Hospital, where he won a choral scholarship so my grandmother was able to pay for his education with sixpence a week, which enabled him to have an egg for breakfast every day. My grandmother taught at a girls' high school in Redland during the day and, travelling on the back of a friend's motorbike, at a night school in Weston-super-Mare. My father and his mother used to holiday in France near Mont Saint-Michel, where my sister now has a house. He was brought up by women and instilled in me a love of the fairer sex. For that and so much more I owe him and my Great-Aunt Molly a great debt of gratitude.

Great-Aunt Molly saw it as her duty to provide for

my father and his future, on her wage as a schools' inspector in the 20s and 30s. I believe she was the first female schools inspector, as I believe her sister was the first female postmistress in the Lake District. Great-Aunt Molly scrimped and saved, making a rabbit last for a week and sitting reading wrapped in a rug rather than light a fire. When she died she left my father 14, The Paragon and enough money to buy a house in Shepton Mallet where he set up in general practice, and to pay for my sister and me to be educated privately.

Algernon Bourke wrote the history of White's Club. And John Bertram Bourke worked in a hospital in Torquay when he was sober, and lived with and was cared for by nuns, who locked him in his room at night. When he died my father was asked to go and talk to the nuns, one of whom was Irish. She told him to make contact with his family in Kanturk, 'And it's stinking rich they are.' This was in 1958. We booked a family holiday at the Bay View Hotel in Waterville. From there, my father wrote a letter to the family and they were quick to respond. The following evening his cousin Hugh drove to Waterville, came into the bar, walked up to my father and said, 'You must be Michael. All of you come with me.'

We drove in convoy to Assolas, just outside Kanturk, where the whole family was there to greet us – we had, as I have always told it, ninety-nine relations. We were welcomed in style, wined and dined, and in the hall, with the help of a grand piano, everyone performed their party pieces.

Assolas became a top gourmet hotel, run by Hugh's son Matthew and his wife. Thirty years ago, just before they opened, Mum and Dad, Britt and Poppy and I went to stay – we were the dress rehearsal. Four or five years ago my sister Sarah and her husband planned to go and stay but Matthew said, 'We don't do that any more.' 'Why not?' 'Because we don't need the money.'

I like to think of that as my grandfather's legacy.

Fifty Years

FIFTY YEARS AFTER playing Puck at RADA I found myself playing Oberon at the Globe, with a brilliant cast of young actors, all in their twenties and thirties – seven beautiful women and three handsome men. To be sixty-nine and able to work with such young talent when my contemporaries in 'proper jobs' have retired makes me feel very privileged. And the fun! Gosh, the fun – which communicated to the audience, who flocked and filled every performance, some returning several times. An older actor said to me when I was in my thirties, 'Listen and learn from the young' – how right he proved to be.

The young actors today all have second jobs, as personal trainers, teachers, scriptwriters. They are never work-shy. Until 1986 Equity was a closed shop and there was reasonably well-paid work for all who were good enough.

I earned my living as an actor until 1986 with

PB (© Antony Dufort).

sidelines in busking, window cleaning and selling planted window boxes door to door. In 1986 I had paid for my house in Brixton and bought the next-door house on a loan, selling it ten years later when the loan was paid off by rental income. I started a property business which has become my pension and provided my daughters Emily and Poppy with somewhere to live. It has also enabled me to choose my work in the theatre and not to feel out of work when I am.

Another actor once said to me, 'Always remember, actors are ten a penny, but good actors, *really* good actors, are nine a penny.'

It's been wonderful – and once this lockdown is over and Covid-19 is under control I have been offered another season of Shakespeare at the Globe. Fingers crossed for the rest of 2021.

Thank you, dear reader, for what you have read of my reminiscences.

Stop me if I've told you this before!

R E A

Acknowledgements

With thanks to Rupert for the suggestion and encouragement, Henrietta for interpreting my scrawl in fountain pen (and correcting the spelling) and editor Sam Carter for making it look fab. Tristram Kenton took the front-cover photograph and Poppy Bourke designed the back cover. Thanks to Antony Dufort for the drawings.

And to Britt, Emily and Poppy and all who have heard many of these stories many times.

Picture Credits

Picture credits where not shown: photographs on pp. vi, x, 22, 35, 45, 111, 117, 164 © and with kind permission of Nobby Clark/ArenaPAL.

P. 92 © and with kind permission of Tim McGuinness/Mirropix/Reach Licensing; p. 135 © and with kind permission of Arthur Sidley/ Mirropix/Reach Licensing; pp. 31, 97, 105 © and with kind permission of Mirropix/Reach Licensing.

P. 101 and front cover © and with kind permission of Tristram Kenton.

Patricia Routledge by Hattie Miles, courtesy of Penny Wesson Management.

Paul Scofield image by Allan Warren, reproduced under Creative Commons Attribution-Share Alike 3.0 Unported licence. Other images from open sources and author's collection.

Antony Dufort has asserted his right under the Copyright, Designs and Patents Act 1988 to be identified as the author of the works so credited.